GW01157914

Key to Ma

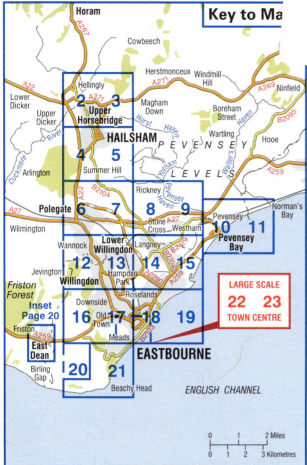

Map area key (panel numbers):

Horam · Cowbeech · Hellingly · Herstmonceux · Windmill Hill · Ninfield · Lower Dicker · Upper Dicker · **2** · A271 · **3** · Magham Down · Boreham Street · B2095 · HAILSHAM · Hurst Haven · Haven · PEVENSEY · Wartling · Hooe · **4** · **5** · Summer Hill · LEVELS · Arlington · Cuckmere River · Rickney · Pevensey Haven · Yotham · Walter's Haven · A259 · Polegate · **6** · **7** · **8** · **9** · Pevensey · Norman's Bay · Wilmington · Stone Cross · Westham · **10** · **11** · Wannock · Lower Willingdon · Langney · Pevensey Bay · Jevington · **12** · **13** · **14** · **15** · Hampden Park · Willingdon · Roselands · Friston Forest · Downside · Old Town · **16** · **17** · **18** · **19** · Inset Page 20 · Friston · A259 · East Dean · Meads · EASTBOURNE · Birling Gap · **20** · **21** · Beachy Head · ENGLISH CHANNEL

LARGE SCALE
22   23
TOWN CENTRE

0 — 1 — 2 Miles
0 — 1 — 2 — 3 Kilometres

Key / Legend

Proposed	
B Road	B2103
Dual Carriageway	
One Way Street — Traffic flow on A Roads is indicated by a heavy line on the drivers' left	
Pedestrianized Road	
Restricted Access	
Track	
Footpath	
Residential Walkway	
Railway	Level Crossing / Station
Built Up Area	MILL ST.
Local Authority Boundary	
Postcode Boundary	
Map Continuation	8
Map Continuation on Large Scale	18
Car Park	P
Church or Chapel	†
Fire Station	■
Hospital	H
Information Centre	i
National Grid Reference	565
Police Station	▲
Post Office	★
Toilet with Facilities for the Disabled	▽

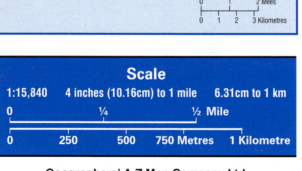

Scale

1:15,840   4 inches (10.16cm) to 1 mile   6.31cm to 1 km

0 — ¼ — ½ Mile

0 — 250 — 500 — 750 Metres — 1 Kilometre

Geographers' A-Z Map Company Ltd.

Head Office : Fairfield Road, Borough Green, Sevenoaks, Kent TN15 8PP Tel: 01732 781000

Showrooms : 44 Gray's Inn Road, London WC1X 8HX Tel: 0171 242 9246

Based upon the Ordnance Survey mapping with the permission of the Controller of Her Majesty's Stationery Office. © Crown Copyright (399000).

EDITION 2 1999 Copyright. © Geographers' A-Z Map Co. Ltd.

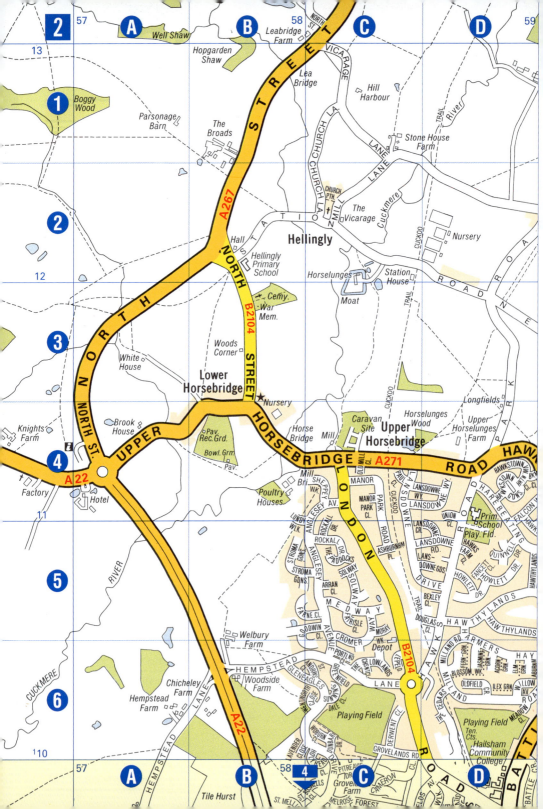

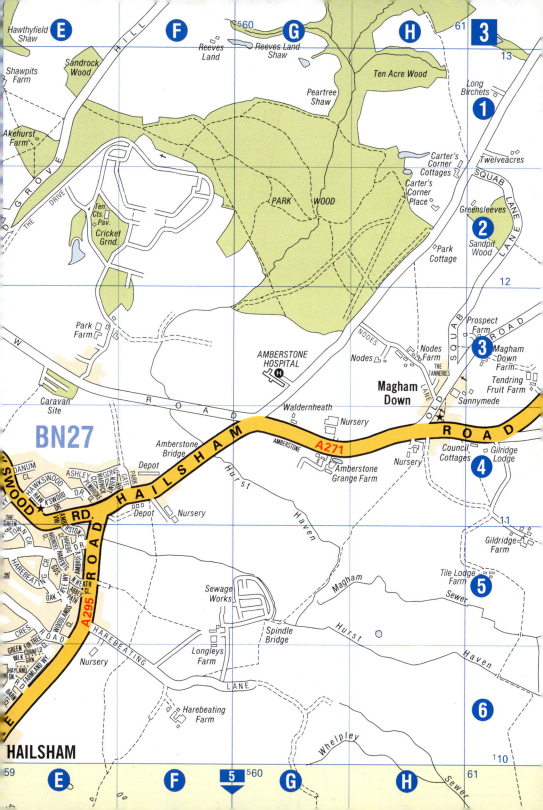

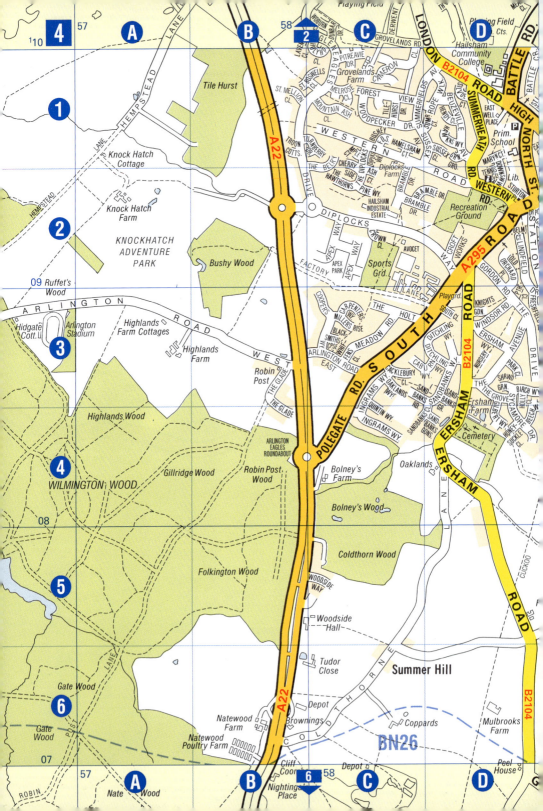

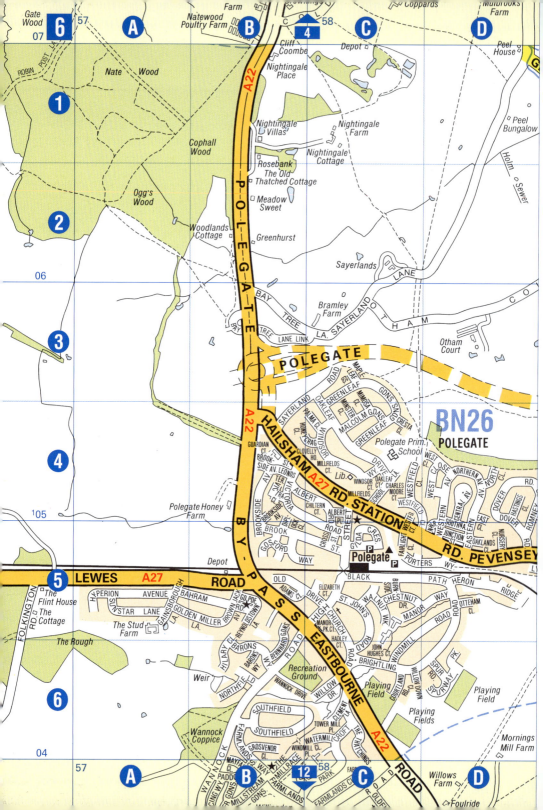

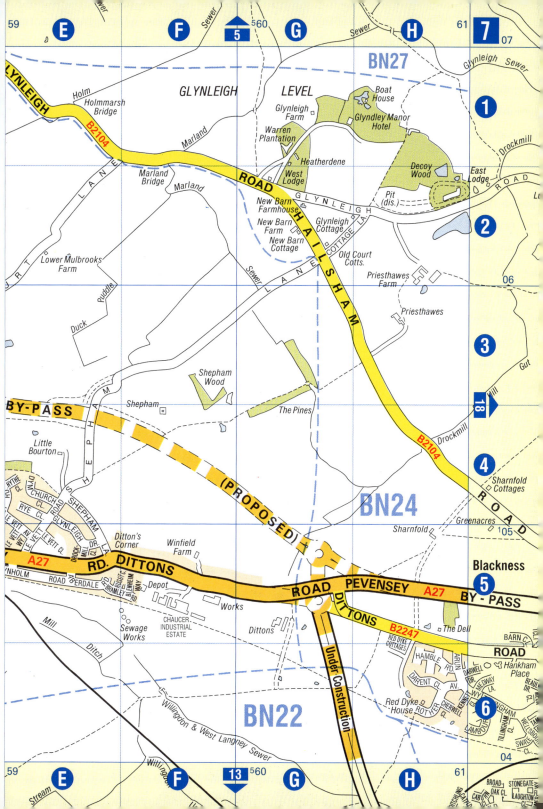

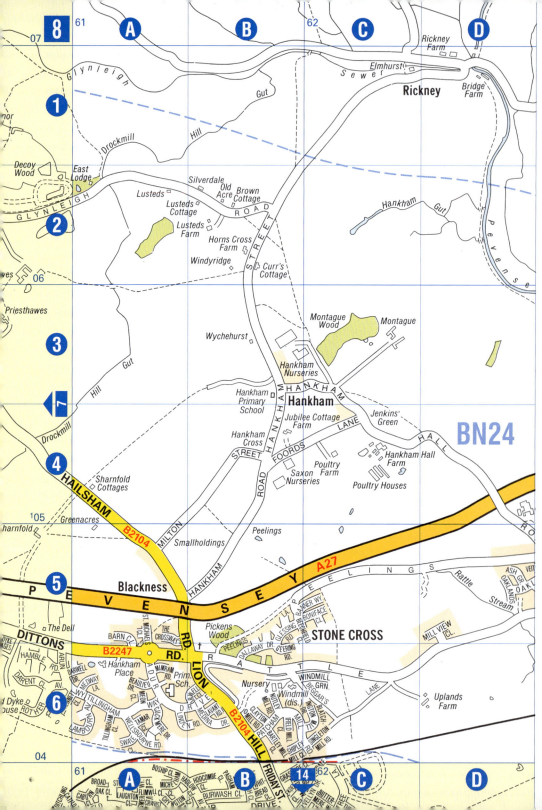

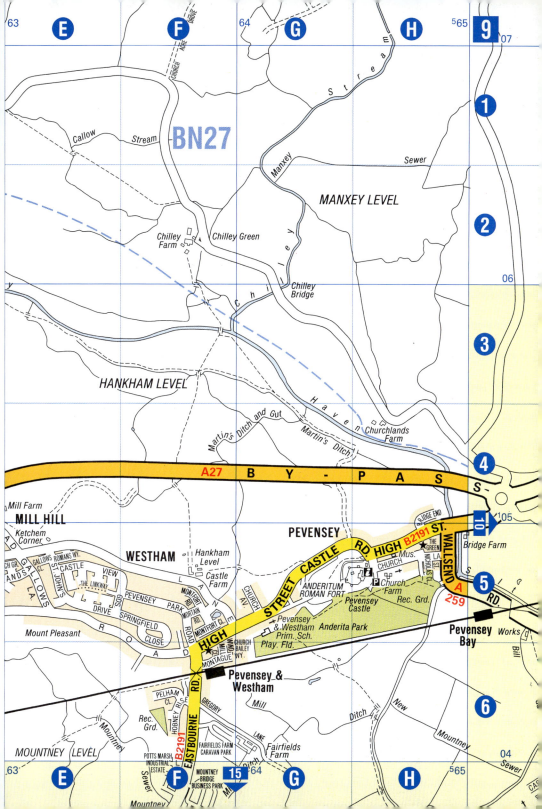

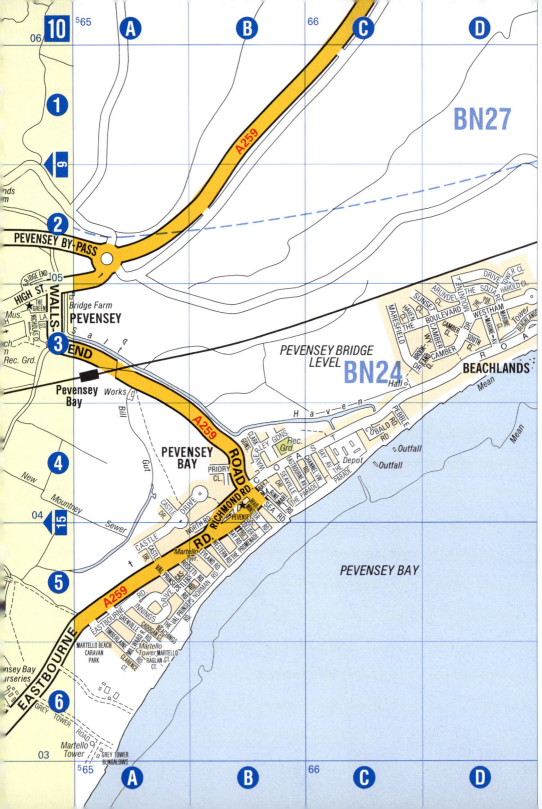

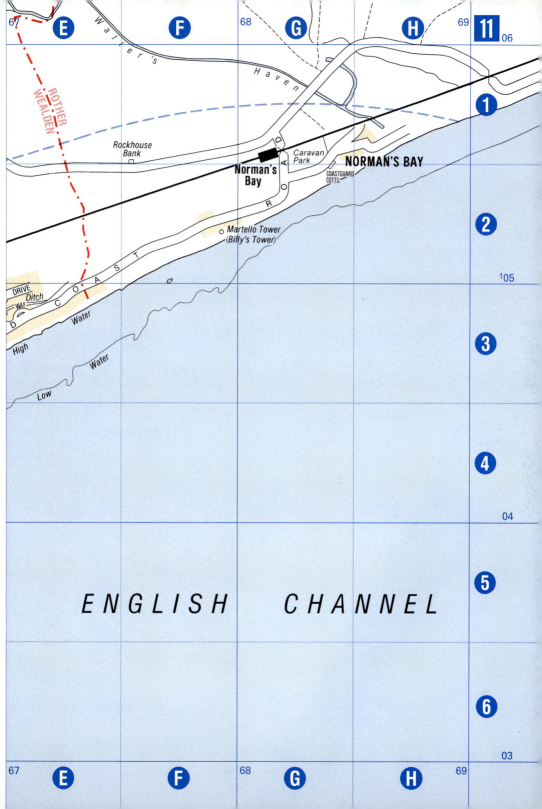

Walter's

Haven

ROTHER
WEALDEN

Rockhouse
Bank

Caravan
Park

Norman's
Bay

NORMAN'S BAY

COASTGUARD
COTTS

○ *Martello Tower*
(Billy's Tower)

C O A S T

DRIVE

Ditch

WAY

D

High   Water

Water

Low

E N G L I S H   C H A N N E L

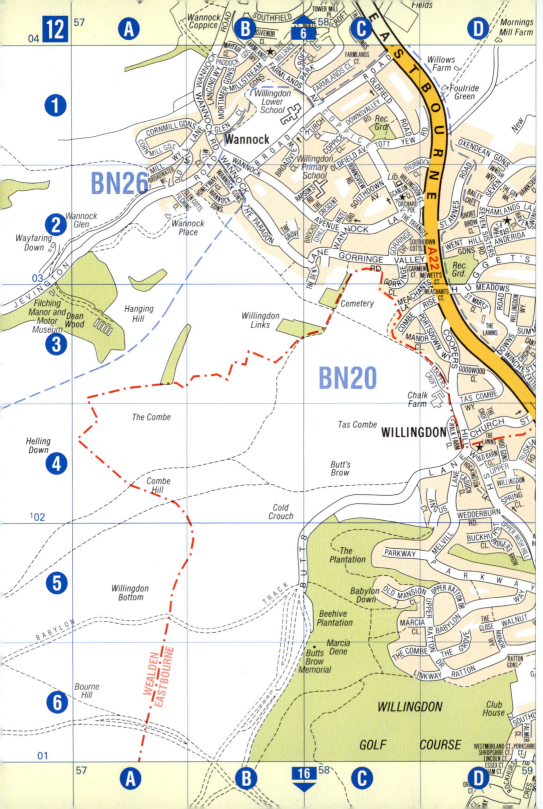

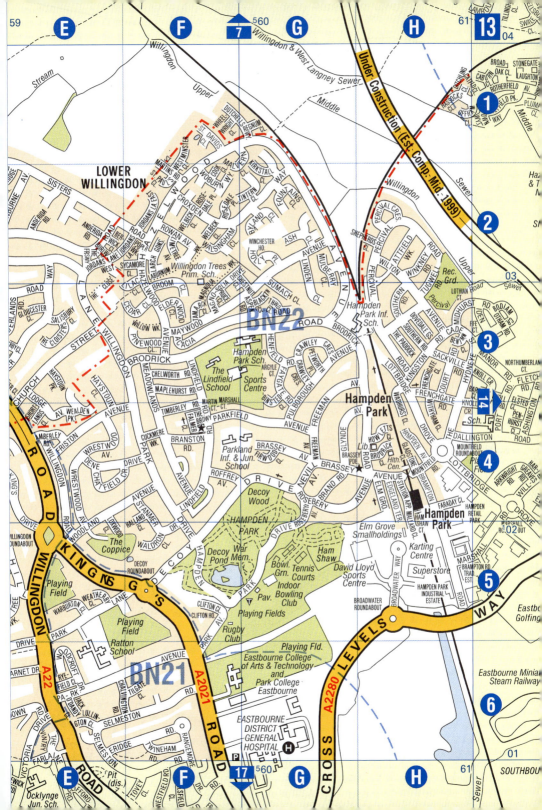

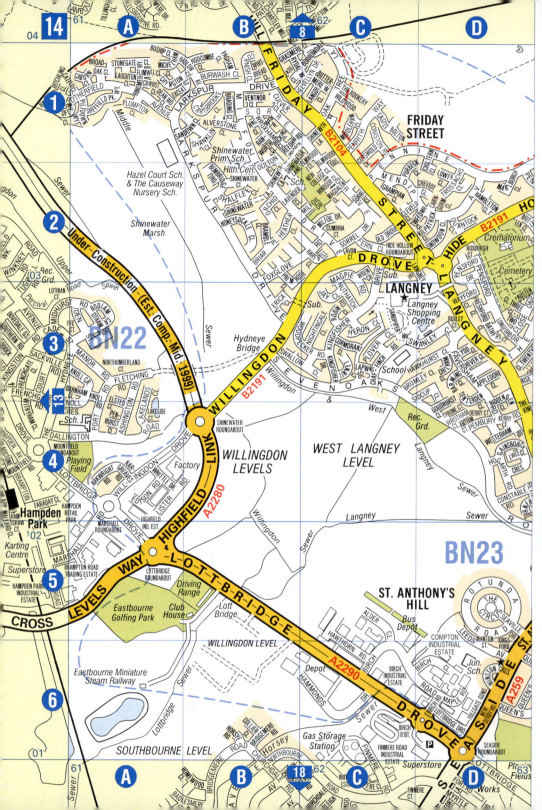

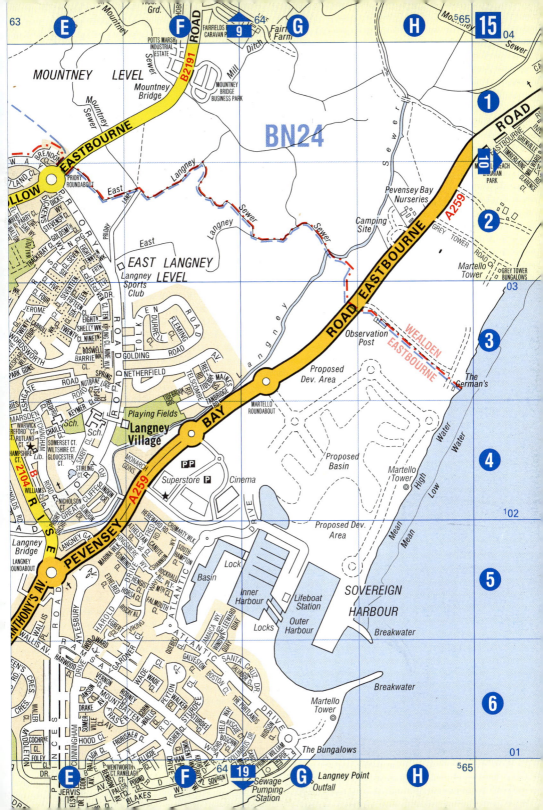

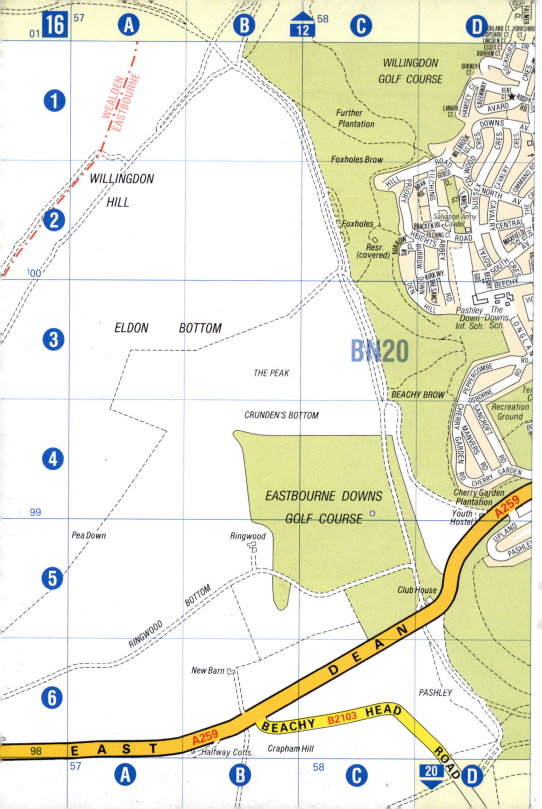

1

WEALDEN
EASTBOURNE

WILLINGDON GOLF COURSE

Further
Plantation

WILLINGDON

HILL

Foxholes Brow

ORLAND CT.
YORKSHIRE
C.T.
SHROPSHIRE CT.
LINCOLN CT.
ESSEX CT.
DURHAM CT.
ORKNEY
CRES.
AVARD
KENT
CT.
RUSPER
RD.
GREENWAY
HAMSEY CL.
LANARK
CT.
DOWNS
AVARD
AV.
MILLBROOK
CRES.
COLWOOD
CRES.
CRES.
NORTH
CAVALRY
AV.
SUSSEX
AV.
COMMAND RD.
THE
CENTRAL
AV.
MAYFIELD
AV.

2

100

Foxholes

Resr.
(covered)

Salvation Army
Citadel

BRACKEN RD.
FILCHING CT.

ROAD

SOUTH
CRES.

3

ELDON BOTTOM

THE PEAK

BURROW DN. CL.
BURROW DOWN
KIRK WY.
DEN HILL
WISANCY RD.

BN20

BEECHY

VIC

Pashley
The
Down- Downs
Inf. Sch. Sch.

BEACHY BROW

LONGLA

RD.

PEPPERCOMBE

RD.

CRUNDEN'S BOTTOM

OSBORNE

Recreation
Ground

Ter
C

4

CHERRY
GARDEN

SANCROFT

MANVERS

RD.

RD.

99

EASTBOURNE DOWNS

GOLF COURSE

Cherry Garden
Plantation

CHERRY GARDEN

A259

Pea Down

Ringwood

Youth
Hostel

UPLAND

PASHLE

5

Club House

RINGWOOD BOTTOM

DEAN

A259

6

New Barn

PASHLEY

BEACHY
A259
B2103
HEAD
ROAD

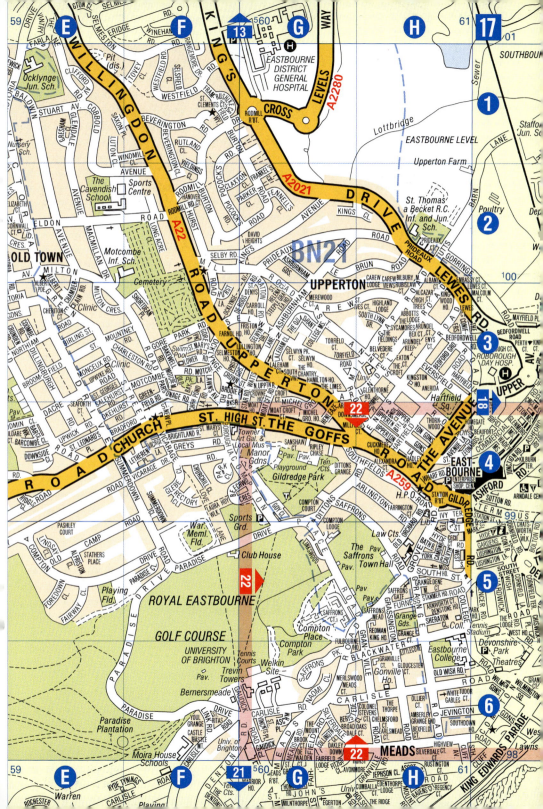

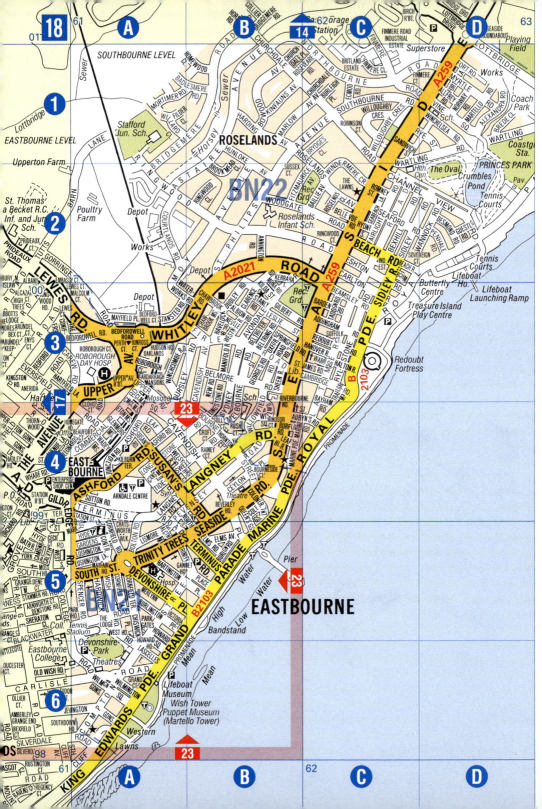

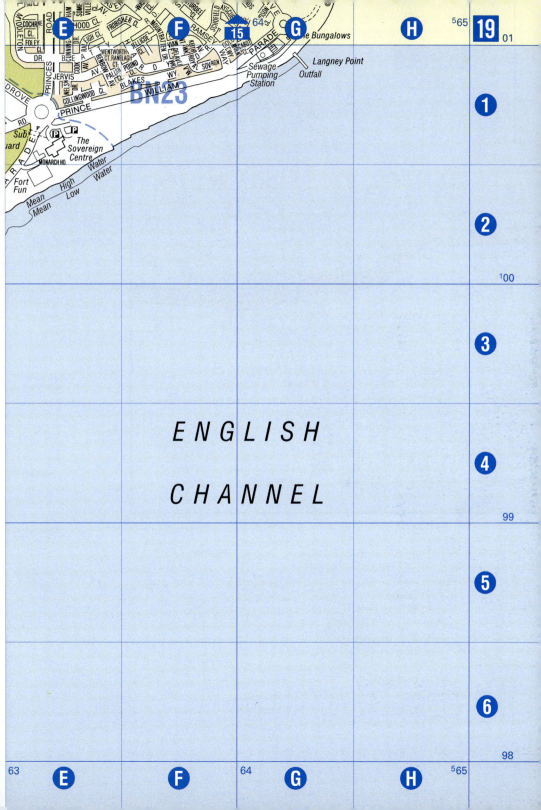

MIDDLETON
COCHRNE CL.
FOLEY CL.
DR.
GUNNING
COOK AV.
RD
Sub
Guard
Fort
Fun

PRINCES
JERVIS
WELSH DR.
COLLINGWOOD CL.

ROAD
WENTWORTH
RANELAGH
CT.
POUND
PALSH
BLAKES
PRINCE
WILLIAM

FROBISHER CL.
MONTBATTEN DR.
SOVRGN

RAMSET
KEITH
ROYAL
PARADE

The
Sovereign
Centre
MONARCH HO.

Le Bungalows
Sewage
Pumping
Station
Langney Point
Outfall

BN23

High   Water
Low   Water
Mean
Mean

The Sovereign Centre area labels:
P P

1

⁵65

2

¹00

3

4

99

ENGLISH

CHANNEL

5

6

98

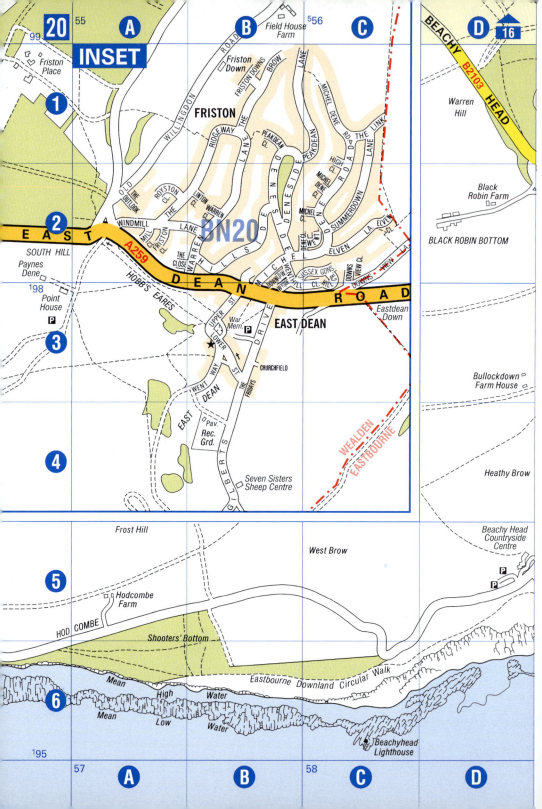

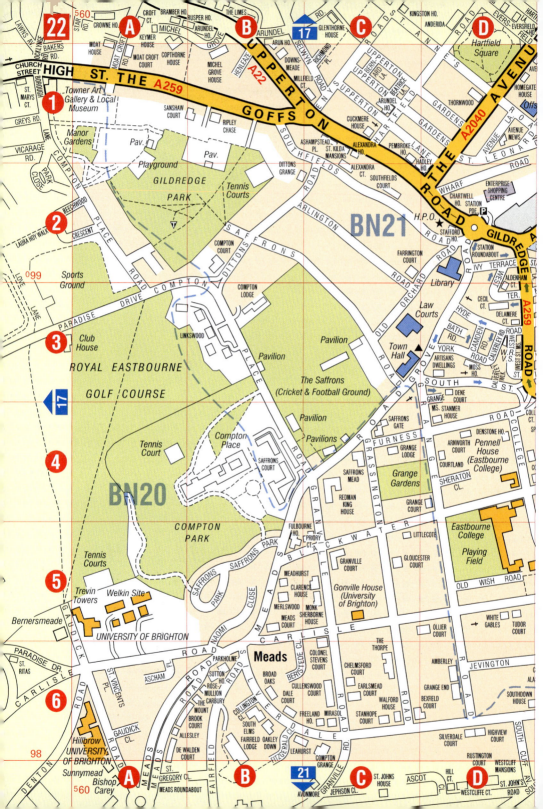

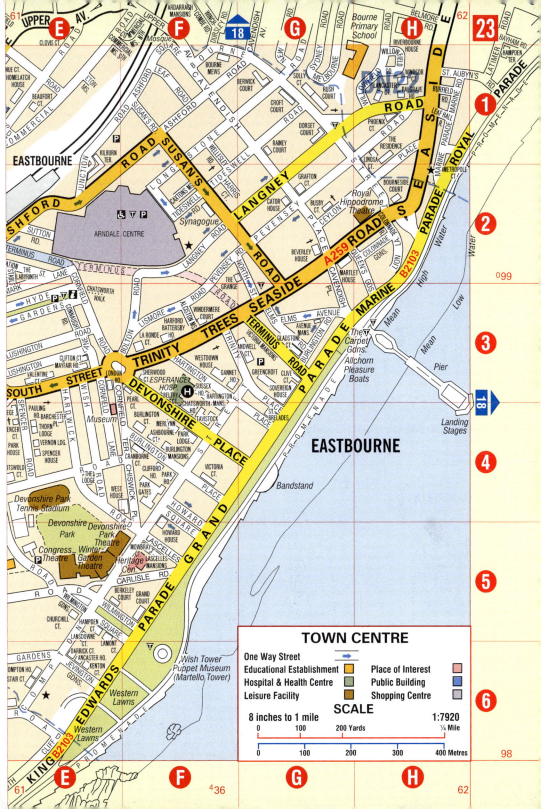

EASTBOURNE

EASTBOURNE

ARNDALE CENTRE

Synagogue

Royal Hippodrome Theatre

The Carpet Gdns.

Allchorn Pleasure Boats

Pier

Landing Stages

Bandstand

Devonshire Park Tennis Stadium

Devonshire Park Theatre

Devonshire Park Winter Garden Theatre

Congress Theatre

Heritage Cen.

Museum

Wish Tower Puppet Museum (Martello Tower)

Western Lawns

Western Lawns

Bourne Primary School

Riverbourne House

TOWN CENTRE

One Way Street	→	
Educational Establishment		Place of Interest
Hospital & Health Centre		Public Building
Leisure Facility		Shopping Centre

SCALE

8 inches to 1 mile   1:7920

0   100   200 Yards   ¼ Mile

0   100   200   300   400 Metres

INDEX TO STREETS

Including Industrial Estates and a selection of Subsidiary Addresses.

HOW TO USE THIS INDEX

1. Each street name is followed by its Posttown or Postal Locality, and then by its map reference; e.g. Abbey Rd. *Eastb* —2D **16** is in the Eastbourne Posttown and is to be found in square 2D on page **16**. The page number being shown in bold type.
A strict alphabetical order is followed in which Av., Rd., St., etc. (though abbreviated) are read in full and as part of the street name; e.g Ash Gro. appears after Ashgate Rd. but before Ashington Rd.

2. Streets and a selection of Subsidary names not shown on the Maps, appear in the index in *Italics* with the thoroughfare to which it is connected shown in brackets; e.g. *Archery Ct. Eastb* —1C **18** *(off Willoughby Cres.)*

3. The page references shown in brackets indicate those streets that appear on the Eastbourne Town Centre map pages 22-23; e.g. Amberley. *Eastb* —6H **17** (6D **22**) is to be found in square 6H on page **17** and also appears on the Town Centre map in square 6D on page **22**.

GENERAL ABBREVIATIONS

All : Alley	Cres : Crescent	La : Lane	St : Saint
App : Approach	Cft : Croft	Lit : Little	II : Second
Arc : Arcade	Dri : Drive	Lwr : Lower	VII : Seventh
Av : Avenue	E : East	Mc : Mac	Shop : Shopping
Bk : Back	VIII : Eighth	Mnr : Manor	VI : Sixth
Boulevd : Boulevard	Embkmt : Embankment	Mans : Mansions	S : South
Bri : Bridge	Est : Estate	Mkt : Market	Sq : Square
B'way : Broadway	Fld : Field	Mdw : Meadow	Sta : Station
Bldgs : Buildings	V : Fifth	M : Mews	St : Street
Bus : Business	I : First	Mt : Mount	Ter : Terrace
Cvn : Caravan	IV : Fourth	N : North	III : Third
Cen : Centre	Gdns : Gardens	Pal : Palace	Trad : Trading
Chu : Church	Gth : Garth	Pde : Parade	Up : Upper
Chyd : Churchyard	Ga : Gate	Pk : Park	Va : Vale
Circ : Circle	Gt : Great	Pas : Passage	Vw : View
Cir : Circus	Grn : Green	Pl : Place	Vs : Villas
Clo : Close	Gro : Grove	Quad : Quadrant	Wlk : Walk
Comn : Common	Ho : House	Res : Residential	W : West
Cotts : Cottages	Ind : Industrial	Ri : Rise	Yd : Yard
Ct : Court	Junct : Junction	Rd : Road	

POSTTOWN AND POSTAL LOCALITY ABBREVIATIONS

Amb : Amberstone	*Fris* : Friston	*Mag D* : Magham Down	*Rat* : Ratton
Blnds : Beachlands	*Hail* : Hailsham	*Old T* : Old Town	*Sto X* : Stone Cross
B Head : Beachy Head	*Hank* : Hankham	*Pev* : Pevensey	*Wart* : Wartling
Eastb : Eastbourne	*Hell* : Hellingly	*Pev B* : Pevensey Bay	*W'ham* : Westham
E Dean : East Dean	*Hers* : Herstmonceux	*Pol* : Polegate	*Will* : Willingdon

INDEX TO STREETS

Abbey Path. *Hail* —5E **3**
Abbey Rd. *Eastb* —2D **16**
Abbotts Lodge. *Eastb* —3H **17**
Aberdale Rd. *Pol* —5E **7**
Acacia Rd. *Eastb* —3F **13**
Acorn Grn. *Hail* —6D **2**
Adams M. *Eastb* —3H **17**
Addingham Rd. *Eastb*
—3C **18**
Adur Dri. *Sto X* —6A **8**
Alastair Ct. *Eastb* —6D **22**
Albert Pde. *Eastb* —3E **17**
Albert Pl. *Pol* —4C **6**
Albert Rd. *Pol* —4B **6**
Albert Ter. *Eastb* —2E **17**
Albion Rd. *Eastb* —3B **18**
Alcazar Ct. *Eastb* —3H **17**
Alciston M. *Eastb* —3F **23**
Aldenham Ct. *Eastb* —3D **22**
Alder Clo. *Eastb* —5C **14**
Alexandra Ct. *Eastb* —2C **22**
Alexandra Ho. *Eastb* —1C **22**
Alexandra Rd. *Eastb* —1D **18**
Alfred Rd. *Eastb* —5F **15**
Alfriston Clo. *Eastb* —5E **17**
Allesley. *Eastb* —6A **22**
Allfrey Rd. *Eastb* —1D **18**

Alverstone Clo. *Eastb* —1B **14**
Amberley. *Eastb*
—6H **17** (6D **22**)
Amberley Rd. *Eastb* —4E **13**
Amberstone. *Hail* —4G **3**
Amberstone Vw. *Hail* —5E **3**
Ancaster Rd. *Eastb* —6E **23**
Anderida Rd. *Eastb* —2D **12**
Andwell Ct. *Eastb* —3G **23**
Anderida. *Eastb*
—3H **17** (1D **22**)
Anglesey Av. *Hail* —5C **2**
Angus Clo. *Eastb* —4D **12**
Annington Rd. *Eastb* —2B **18**
Anson Clo. *Eastb* —6E **15**
Antares Path. *Hail* —2G **5**
Antrim Ct. *Eastb* —4D **14**
Apex Pk. *Hail* —2C **4**
Apex Way. *Hail* —2C **4**
Appledore Clo. *Eastb* —3D **14**
Archery Ct. Eastb —1C **18**
(off Willoughby Cres.)
Archery Wlk. *Hail* —2E **5**
Ardarragh Mans. *Eastb*
—3A **18** (1F **23**)
Argyle Ct. *Eastb* —3G **13**
Arkwright Rd. *Eastb* —4A **14**

Arlington Ho. Eastb —3G **17**
(off Upperton Rd.)
Arlington Rd. *Eastb*
—4H **17** (2C **22**)
Arlington Rd. E. *Hail* —3C **4**
Arlington Rd. W. *Hail* —3A **4**
Arndale Cen. *Eastb*
—4A **18** (2E **23**)
Arnworth Ct. *Eastb*
—5H **17** (4D **22**)
Arran Clo. *Hail* —5C **2**
Artisans Dwellings. *Eastb*
—3D **22**
Arundel Clo. *Hail* —5E **3**
Arundel Clo. *Pev B* —3D **10**
Arundel Ct. *Eastb* —3H **17**
Arundel Ho. *Eastb* —1B **22**
(nr. Michel Gro.)
Arundel Ho. *Eastb* —1C **22**
(nr. Upperton Gdns.)
Arundel Keep. *Eastb* —3H **17**
Arundel Rd. *Eastb*
—3H **17** (1B **22**)
Arun Ho. *Eastb* —4G **17** (1B **22**)
Arun Way. *Sto X* —6H **7**
Ascham Pl. *Eastb*
—6G **17** (6A **22**)

Ascot Clo. *Eastb*
—1H **21** (6C **22**)
Ashampstead Pl. *Eastb* —1C **22**
Ashbourne Ct. *Eastb* —4F **23**
Ashburnham Gdns. *Eastb*
—2G **17**
Ashburnham Pl. *Hail* —5C **2**
Ashburnham Rd. *Eastb* —3G **17**
Ash Clo. *Eastb* —2G **13**
Ash Ct. *Hail* —2C **4**
Ashford Clo. *Hail* —2E **5**
Ashford Rd. *Eastb*
—4A **18** (2E **23**)
Ashford Sq. *Eastb*
—4A **18** (1F **23**)
Ashgate Rd. *Eastb* —3E **15**
Ash Gro. *W'ham* —5D **8**
Ashington Rd. *Eastb* —4A **14**
Ashley Gdns. *Amb* —4E **3**
Ashley Gdns. Eastb —1C **18**
(off Willoughby Cres.)
Aspen Rd. *Eastb* —3G **13**
Astaire Av. *Eastb* —2B **18**
Athelstan Clo. *Eastb* —5F **15**
Atlantic Dri. *Eastb* —5F **15**
Attfield Wlk. *Eastb* —2H **13**
Austen Wlk. *Eastb* —3D **14**

Avard Cres. *Eastb* —1D **16**
Avenue Ct. *Eastb* —1D **22**
Avenue La. *Eastb*
—4H **17** (1D **22**)
Avenue Mans. *Eastb* —3G **23**
Avenue M. *Eastb* —1D **22**
Avenue, The. *Eastb*
—4H **17** (2D **22**)
Avenue, The. *Hail* —3D **4**
Avocet. *Hail* —2C **4**
Avon Ct. *Eastb* —2C **14**
Avondale Rd. *Eastb* —3B **18**
Avonmore. *Eastb*
—1G **21** (6B **22**)
Aylesbury Av. *Eastb* —5E **15**
Ayscue Clo. *Eastb* —6F **15**

Babylon Track. *Eastb* —5A **12**
Babylon Way. *Eastb* —5D **12**
Badgers Brow. *Eastb* —5D **12**
Badlesmere Rd. *Eastb* —1A **18**
Bahram Rd. *Pol* —5B **6**
Bailey Cres. *Eastb* —2D **12**
Baillie Av. *Eastb* —2C **18**
Bakers Rd. *Eastb*
—4F **17** (1A **22**)
Bakewell Rd. *Eastb* —3F **17**
Baldwin Av. *Eastb* —1E **17**
Banner Way. *Sto X* —5B **8**
Barchester Pl. *Eastb* —4E **23**
Barcombe Clo. *Eastb* —4E **17**
Barcombe Wlk. *Eastb* —4E **17**
Barden Rd. *Eastb* —3C **18**
Barming Clo. *Eastb* —3D **14**
Barn Clo. *Hail* —6E **3**
Barn Clo. *Sto X* —5A **8**
Barnham Clo. *Eastb* —3A **14**
Barons Way. *Pol* —6B **6**
Barrie Clo. *Eastb* —3E **15**
Bartley Mill Clo. *Sto X* —6B **8**
Baslow Rd. *Eastb* —2F **21**
Bathford Clo. *Eastb* —3D **14**
Bath Rd. *Eastb* —5H **17** (3D **22**)
Battle Cres. *Hail* —1D **4**
Battle Rd. *Hail* —1D **4**
Bay Av. *Pev B* —4C **10**
Bayham Rd. *Eastb*
—3C **18** (1H **23**)
Bayham Rd. *Hail* —2F **5**
Bay Pond Rd. *Eastb* —3F **17**
Bay Rd. *Pev B* —5B **10**
Bay Ter. *Pev B* —4B **10**
Bay Tree La. *Pol* —3B **6**
Bay Tree La. Link. *Pol* —3B **6**
Beachings, The. *Pev B* —5A **10**
Beachlands Way. *Pev* —3D **10**
Beach M. *Eastb* —2C **18**
Beach Rd. *Eastb* —2C **18**
Beachy Head Rd. *B Head*
—6B **16**
Beamsley Rd. *Eastb* —3C **18**
Beatrice La. *Eastb*
—4H **17** (1C **22**)
Beatty Rd. *Eastb* —1E **19**
Beaufort Ct. *Eastb*
—4A **18** (1E **23**)
Beaulieu Dri. *Pev* —6A **8**
Beckenham Clo. *Hail* —4D **2**
Bedford Gro. *Eastb* —3H **17**
Bedfordwell Ct. *Eastb* —3A **18**
Bedfordwell Rd. *Eastb* —3H **17**
Bedfordwell Roundabout. Eastb
(off Bedfordwell Rd.) —3A **18**
Beechfield Clo. *Sto X* —5B **8**
Beechwood Clo. *Hail* —4D **4**
Beechwood Cres. *Eastb*
—4F **17** (2A **22**)

Beechy Av. *Eastb* —3D **16**
Beechy Gdns. *Eastb* —2D **16**
Beggar's La. *Pev* —6C **8**
Belfry, The. *Hail* —1C **4**
Bell Banks Rd. *Hail* —2E **5**
Belle Vue Ct. Eastb —2C **18**
(off Belle Vue Rd.)
Belle Vue Rd. *Eastb* —2C **18**
Belmont St. *Hail* —2D **4**
Belmore Rd. *Eastb*
—3B **18** (1H **23**)
Beltring Rd. *Eastb* —3B **18**
Beltring Ter. *Eastb* —3B **18**
Beltry Ct. *Eastb* —3F **23**
Belvedere Ct. *Eastb* —3H **17**
Bembridge Rd. *Eastb* —2B **14**
Benbow Av. *Eastb* —1E **19**
Benjamin Clo. *Eastb* —3H **13**
Beristede Clo. *Eastb*
—6G **17** (6B **22**)
Berkeley Ct. *Eastb* —5E **23**
Berkeley Wlk. Eastb —2E **15**
(off Close Seventeen)
Berkshire Ct. Eastb —3B **18**
(off Leslie St.)
Bernard La. *Eastb*
—4H **17** (1C **22**)
Bernhard Gdns. *Pol* —6B **6**
Berwick Clo. *Eastb* —2E **13**
Berwick Ct. *Eastb* —1G **23**
Beuzeville Av. *Hail* —1D **4**
Beverington Clo. *Eastb* —1F **17**
Beverington Rd. *Eastb* —1F **17**
Beverley Ho. *Eastb*
—4B **18** (2G **23**)
Bex Ct. *Eastb* —3H **17**
Bexfield Ct. *Eastb*
—6H **17** (6D **22**)
Bexhill Rd. *Eastb* —2C **18**
Bexley Clo. *Hail* —5D **2**
Biddenden Clo. *Eastb* —3D **14**
Bilbury M. *Eastb* —2H **17**
Binsted Clo. *Eastb* —3G **13**
Birch Clo. *Eastb* —6D **14**
Birch Ind. Est. *Eastb* —6C **14**
Birch Rd. *Eastb* —6C **14**
Birch Roundabout. Eastb
—6C **14**
Birch Way. *Hail* —3D **4**
Birling St. *Eastb* —3E **17**
Biscay Av. *Eastb* —5F **15**
Black Path. *Pol* —5C **6**
Blacksmiths Copse. *Hail* —3C **4**
Blackthorn Clo. *Eastb* —3G **13**
Blackwater Rd. *Eastb*
—6H **17** (5B **22**)
Blakes Way. *Eastb* —1F **19**
Blatchington Mill Dri. Pev
—6C **8**
Blenheim Way. *Pol* —5F **7**
Blossom Wlk. *Hail* —6D **2**
Bodiam Cres. *Eastb* —3A **14**
Bodmin Clo. *Eastb* —4E **17**
Bolsover Rd. *Eastb* —1H **21**
Bolton Rd. *Eastb*
—5A **18** (3F **23**)
Boniface Clo. *Sto X* —5C **8**
Borough La. *Eastb*
—4F **17** (1A **22**)
Borrowdale Clo. *Eastb* —4E **17**
Boscawen Clo. *Eastb* —6F **15**
Boship Clo. *Eastb* —1A **14**
Boston Clo. *Eastb* —6F **15**
Boswell Wlk. *Eastb* —3E **15**
Boulevard, The. *Pev B* —3C **10**
Bourne M. *Eastb* —1F **23**
Bourneside Ct. *Eastb*
—4B **18** (2H **23**)

Bourne St. *Eastb*
—4A **18** (1F **23**)
Bowley Rd. *Hail* —2E **5**
Bowood Av. *Eastb* —1B **18**
Bracken Rd. *Eastb* —2D **16**
(in two parts)
Bradford Ct. Eastb —3B **18**
(off Firle Rd.)
Bradford St. *Eastb* —4E **17**
Brading Clo. *Eastb* —1B **14**
Bramber Ho. *Eastb* —1A **22**
Bramble Clo. *Eastb* —2B **14**
Bramble Dri. *Hail* —2C **4**
Bramley Rd. *Pol* —5E **7**
Brampton Rd. *Eastb* —4H **13**
Brampton Rd. Trad. Est. *Eastb*
—5H **13**
Brand Rd. *Eastb* —4G **13**
Branston Rd. *Eastb* —4F **13**
Brassey Av. *Eastb* —4G **13**
Brassey Pde. *Eastb* —4G **13**
Brede Clo. *Eastb* —1D **18**
Brendon Clo. *Eastb* —1E **15**
Briar Pl. *Eastb* —2B **14**
Bridge End. *Pev* —5H **9**
Bridgemere Rd. *Eastb* —1A **18**
Brightland Rd. *Eastb* —4F **17**
Brightling Rd. *Pol* —6C **6**
Britland Est. *Eastb* —1C **18**
Britten Clo. *Eastb* —2D **14**
Broadoak Clo. *Eastb* —1A **14**
Broad Oaks. *Eastb*
—6G **17** (6B **22**)
Broad Rd. *Eastb* —1B **12**
Broadview Clo. *Eastb* —2B **12**
Broadwater Roundabout. Eastb
—5H **13**
Broadwater Way. *Eastb* —5H **13**
Broadway, The. *Eastb* —4F **13**
Brocks Ghyll. *Eastb* —2C **12**
Brodie Pl. *Eastb* —3F **17**
Brodrick Clo. *Eastb* —4H **13**
Brodrick Rd. *Eastb* —3F **13**
Bromley Clo. *Eastb* —3C **14**
Brook Ct. *Eastb*
—6G **17** (6B **22**)
Brookland Clo. *Pev B* —3C **10**
Brookmead Clo. *Eastb* —2B **18**
Brookside Av. *Pol* —4B **6**
Brook St. *Pol* —5B **6**
Broom Clo. *Eastb* —3F **13**
Broomfield St. *Eastb* —3E **17**
Browning Wlk. Eastb —3E **15**
(off Jerome Clo.)
Brown Jack Av. *Pol* —5B **6**
Brow, The. *Fris* —1B **20**
Brydges Clo. *Eastb* —1C **18**
Buckhurst Clo. *Eastb* —5D **12**
Burfield Rd. *Eastb*
—4B **18** (1H **23**)
Burleigh Pl. *Eastb* —1C **18**
Burlington Ct. *Eastb* —4F **23**
Burlington Mans. *Eastb* —4F **23**
Burlington Pl. *Eastb*
—5A **18** (4F **23**)
Burlington Rd. *Eastb*
—5B **18** (3G **23**)
Burlow Clo. *Eastb* —2E **13**
Burnside. *Pol* —5C **6**
Burnside Ct. Pol —5C **6**
(off Black Path Rd.)
Burrow Down. *Eastb* —2D **16**
Burrow Down Clo. *Eastb*
—2C **16**
Burton Rd. *Eastb* —1F **17**
Burton Wlk. Hail —2D **4**
(off Lindfield Dri.)
Burwash Clo. *Eastb* —1B **14**

Busby Ct. *Eastb* —2G **23**
Bushey Fields. *Hail* —1C **4**
Buttermere Way. *Eastb* —1C **14**
Buttsfield. *Hail* —3E **5**
Butts La. *Eastb* —5B **12**
Buxton Rd. *Eastb* —1G **21**
Bylands Clo. *Eastb* —2G **13**
Byron Wlk. Eastb —2E **15**
(off Rising, The)

Cabot Clo. *Eastb* —6G **15**
Caburn Clo. *Eastb* —1A **14**
Caburn Way. *Hail* —3C **4**
Cacklebury Clo. *Hail* —3C **4**
Cade St. *Eastb* —3H **13**
Cadogan Ct. *Pev* —5A **10**
Cairngorm Clo. *Eastb* —2D **14**
Calverley Rd. *Eastb*
—5H **17** (3D **22**)
Calverley Wlk. *Eastb* —3D **22**
Camber Clo. *Pev B* —3D **10**
Camber Dri. *Pev B* —3D **10**
Camber Way. *Pev B* —3D **10**
Cambridge Rd. *Eastb* —3C **18**
Camden Rd. *Eastb*
—5H **17** (3D **22**)
Cameron Clo. *Hail* —1C **4**
Canterbury Clo. *Eastb* —3D **12**
Canute Clo. *Eastb* —5F **15**
Capella Path. *Hail* —2F **5**
Carew Ct. Eastb
—3H **17** (1D **22**)
(off Hartfield La.)
Carew Lodge. *Eastb* —2H **17**
Carew Rd. *Eastb* —3G **17**
Carew Views. *Eastb* —2H **17**
Carisbrooke Clo. *Eastb* —1B **14**
Carlisle Rd. *Eastb*
—1F **21** (6A **22**)
Carlton Rd. *Eastb* —2C **18**
Carmen Ct. *Eastb* —2C **12**
Carpenters Way. *Hail* —3C **4**
Carriers Path. *Hail* —1D **4**
Carroll Ho. *Eastb* —3G **15**
Carroll Wlk. *Eastb* —3E **15**
Castle Bolton. *Eastb* —1C **14**
Castle Dri. *Pev B* —4A **10**
Castle Mt. *Eastb* —6F **17**
Castle Rd. *Pev* —5G **9**
Castleross Rd. *Pev B* —5A **10**
Castle Vw. Gdns. *W'ham* —5E **9**
Catfield Clo. *Eastb* —1H **13**
Cator Ho. *Eastb* —2G **23**
Cavalry Cres. *Eastb* —2D **16**
Cavendish Av. *Eastb*
—3B **18** (1G **23**)
Cavendish Pl. *Eastb*
—4A **18** (1F **23**)
Caxtons M. *Eastb*
—4A **18** (2F **23**)
Cecil Ct. *Eastb* —5H **17** (3D **22**)
Cedar Clo. *Eastb* —3F **13**
Cedars, The. *Hail* —6D **2**
Central Av. *Eastb* —2D **16**
Central Av. *Pol* —4D **6**
Ceylon Pl. *Eastb*
—4B **18** (2G **23**)
Chaffinch Rd. *Eastb* —3C **14**
Chailey Clo. *Eastb* —4E **15**
Chalk Farm Clo. *Eastb* —4D **12**
Chalvington Ho. Eastb —3F **7**
(off Ocklynge Rd.)
Chalvington Rd. *Eastb* —6E **13**
Chamberlain Rd. *Eastb* —3E **15**
Channel Vw. Rd. *Eastb* —2C **18**
Channel Vw. Rd. *Pev B* —4C **10**
Chantry, The. *Eastb* —3G **17**

Chapel Barn Clo. *Hail* —2E **5**
Charles Moore Ct. *Pol* —4C **6**
Charleston Rd. *Eastb* —3E **17**
Chartwell Ho. *Eastb* —2D **22**
Chatfield Cres. *Eastb* —4E **13**
Chatsworth Gdns. *Eastb*
—1H **21**
Chatsworth Ho. *Eastb* —4F **23**
Chatsworth Wlk. *Eastb*
—5A **18** (3E **23**)
Chaucer Ind. Est. *Pol* —5F **7**
Chaucer Wlk. Eastb —2E **15**
(off Close Seventeen)
Chawbrook M. *Eastb* —3B **18**
Chawbrook Rd. *Eastb* —3B **18**
Chelmsford Ct. *Eastb*
—6H **17** (6C **22**)
Chelworth Rd. *Eastb* —3F **13**
Cheriton Ct. *Eastb* —3E **17**
Cherry Garden Rd. *Eastb*
—4D **16**
Cherry Side. *Hail* —1C **4**
Cherwell Clo. *Sto X* —6H **7**
Cheshire Ct. Eastb —3B **18**
(off Leslie St.)
Chesterfield Gdns. *Eastb*
—1G **21**
Chesterfield Rd. *Eastb* —1G **21**
Chestnut Clo. *Eastb* —2G **13**
Chestnut Clo. *Hail* —6C **2**
Chestnut Dri. *Pol* —5C **6**
Cheviot Clo. *Eastb* —2D **14**
Chichester Clo. *Eastb* —3D **12**
Chilham Clo. *Eastb* —3D **14**
Chiltern Clo. *Eastb* —2D **14**
Chiswick Pl. *Eastb*
—5A **18** (4F **23**)
Church Acre Drove. *Wart* —1F **9**
Church Av. *W'ham* —5G **9**
Church Bailey. *W'ham* —6G **9**
Church Clo. *Eastb* —1C **12**
Churchdale Av. *Eastb* —1C **18**
Churchdale Pl. *Eastb* —1B **18**
Churchdale Rd. *Eastb* —6B **14**
Churchfield. *E Dean* —3B **20**
Churchill Clo. *Eastb* —5E **23**
Churchill Ct. *Eastb* —5E **23**
Church La. *Eastb* —4F **17**
Church La. *Hell* —1C **2**
Church La. *Pev* —5H **9**
Church Path. *Hell* —2C **2**
Church Rd. *Pol* —5C **6**
Church St. *Old T*
—4F **17** (1A **22**)
Church St. *Will* —4D **12**
Chyngton Clo. *Eastb* —1A **14**
Circus, The. *Pev* —6A **10**
Clarence Ct. *Eastb* —5D **14**
Clarence Ho. *Eastb* —5B **22**
Clarence Rd. *Eastb* —3B **18**
Clark Gdns. *Eastb* —3F **15**
Claxton Clo. *Eastb* —2F **17**
Clayton Mill Rd. *Sto X* —6B **8**
Clement La. *Pol* —6C **6**
Cleveland Clo. *Eastb* —2C **14**
Cliff Ho. *Eastb* —1G **21**
Clifford Av. *Eastb* —1E **17**
Clifford Ho. *Eastb* —4F **23**
Cliff Rd. *Eastb* —2G **21**
Clifton Clo. *Eastb* —5F **13**
Clifton Ct. *Eastb* —3E **23**
Clifton Ho. *Eastb* —5F **13**
Clive Ct. *Eastb* —3G **23**
Cloisters, The. *Eastb* —3E **13**
Close Eight. *Eastb* —2E **15**
Close Eighteen. *Eastb* —3E **15**
Close Eleven. *Eastb* —2E **15**
Close Fifteen. *Eastb* —3E **15**

Close Five. *Eastb* —2E **15**
Close Four. *Eastb* —3E **15**
Close Fourteen. *Eastb* —2E **15**
Close Nine. *Eastb* —3E **15**
Close Nineteen. *Eastb* —3E **15**
Close One. *Eastb* —3D **14**
Close Seven. *Eastb* —2E **15**
Close Seventeen. *Eastb* —3E **15**
Close Six. *Eastb* —2E **15**
Close Sixteen. *Eastb* —3E **15**
Close Ten. *Eastb* —3E **15**
Close, The. *Eastb* —3E **13**
(nr. Hugget's La.)
Close, The. *Eastb* —5D **12**
(nr. Manor Way)
Close, The. *E Dean* —2A **20**
Close Three. *Eastb* —3D **14**
Close Twelve. *Eastb* —3E **15**
Close Twenty. *Eastb* —3E **15**
Close Twentyfive. *Eastb*
—3D **14**
Close Twentyfour. *Eastb*
—3E **15**
Close Two. *Eastb* —3D **14**
Clovelly Ho. *Pol* —4C **6**
Clovis Ct. *Eastb*
—4A **18** (1E **23**)
Clyde Pk. *Hail* —2E **5**
Coastgaurd Cotts. *Pev* —2G **11**
Coastguard Sq. Eastb —3C **18**
(off Latimer Rd.)
Coast Rd. *Pev B* —4B **10**
Cobald Rd. *Pev B* —4C **10**
Cobbold Av. *Eastb* —1E **17**
Cobden Pl. Hail —2E **5**
(off Station Rd.)
Cochrane Clo. *Eastb* —6E **15**
Coldthorne La. *Hail* —6B **4**
Coleridge Wlk. Eastb —3F **15**
(off Close Fifteen)
College Ct. *Eastb* —4D **22**
College Ct. Eastb
—5A **18** (4E **23**)
(off Spencer Rd.)
College M. *Eastb* —3G **17**
College Rd. *Eastb*
—5H **17** (4D **22**)
Collier Clo. *Eastb* —6B **14**
Collier Rd. *Pev B* —5B **10**
Collington Clo. *Eastb*
—6G **17** (6B **22**)
Collingwood Clo. *Eastb* —1E **19**
Colonel Stevens Ct. *Eastb*
—6H **17** (6C **22**)
Colonnade Gdns. *Eastb*
—4B **18** (2H **23**)
Colonnade Rd. *Eastb*
—4B **18** (2H **23**)
Coltstocks Rd. *Eastb* —1F **21**
Columbus Dri. *Eastb* —1F **19**
Colville Ct. Eastb —3G **17**
(off Selwyn Rd.)
Colwood Cres. *Eastb* —2D **16**
Combe La. *Eastb* —2F **21**
Combe Ri. *Eastb* —3C **12**
Combe, The. *Eastb* —6C **12**
Command Rd. *Eastb* —2D **16**
Commercial M. N. *Eastb*
—3A **18** (1F **23**)
Commercial M. S. *Eastb*
—4A **18** (1E **23**)
Commercial Rd. *Eastb*
—4A **18** (1E **23**)
Compton Ct. *Eastb*
—4G **17** (2B **22**)
Compton Dri. *Eastb* —5E **17**
Compton Grange. *Eastb*
—6C **22**

Compton Ho. *Eastb* —6E **23**
Compton Ind. Est. *Eastb*
—6D **14**
Compton Lodge. *Eastb*
—5G **17** (3B **22**)
Compton Pl. Rd. *Eastb*
—4G **17** (1A **22**)
Compton St. *Eastb*
—6A **18** (6E **23**)
Compton Ter. *Hail* —3E **5**
Conifers, The. *Eastb* —3H **17**
Coniston Rd. *Eastb* —1C **14**
Connaught Rd. *Eastb*
—5A **18** (3E **23**)
Constable Rd. *Eastb* —4D **14**
Cook Av. *Eastb* —1E **19**
Cook Ho. *Eastb* —3D **14**
Coombe Rd. *Eastb* —3E **17**
Coopers Cft. *Eastb* —3D **12**
Coopers Hill. *Eastb* —3D **12**
Coopers Way. *Hail* —3C **4**
Coppice Av. *Eastb* —1C **12**
Coppice Clo. *Eastb* —1C **12**
Copthorne Ho. *Eastb* —1A **22**
Cormorant Clo. *Eastb* —3C **14**
Cornfield Grn. *Hail* —6E **3**
Cornfield La. *Eastb*
—5A **18** (3E **23**)
Cornfield Rd. *Eastb*
—5A **18** (2E **23**)
Cornfield Ter. *Eastb*
—5A **18** (3E **23**)
Cornish Clo. *Eastb* —1B **14**
Cornmill Gdns. *Pol* —1A **12**
Cornwall Ct. *Eastb* —2E **17**
Cornwallis Clo. *Eastb* —6F **15**
Cotswold Clo. *Eastb* —1C **14**
Cotswold Ct. *Eastb* —4E **23**
Cottage La. *Hank* —2G **7**
Courtland. *Eastb* —4D **22**
Courtland Rd. *Pol* —6C **6**
Courtlands Rd. *Eastb* —2A **18**
Court Rd. *Eastb* —3H **13**
Coventry Ct. Eastb —1D **18**
(off Allfrey Rd.)
Cranborne Av. *Eastb* —1E **21**
Cranborne Ct. *Eastb* —4F **23**
Crawley Cres. *Eastb* —3G **13**
Crescent, The. *Eastb* —2D **16**
Crescent, The. *Will* —2C **12**
Cresta Clo. *Pol* —4C **6**
Croft Clo. *Pol* —1B **12**
Croft Ct. *Eastb*
—4B **18** (1G **23**)
(nr. Bourne St.)
Croft Ct. *Eastb*
—3G **17** (1A **22**)
(nr. Moat Cft. Rd.)
Croft, The. *Eastb* —3H **17**
Croft, The. *Will* —4D **12**
Croft Works. *Hail* —2D **4**
Cromarty Wlk. *Eastb* —5F **15**
Cromer Way. *Hail* —5C **2**
Cross Levels Way. *Eastb*
—1G **17**
Cross St. *Pol* —5C **6**
Crossways, The. *Sto X* —5A **8**
Crouch Clo. *Eastb* —4D **12**
Crowhurst Clo. *Eastb* —1A **14**
Crown Clo. *Eastb* —2C **4**
Crowne Ho. *Eastb*
—3G **17** (1A **22**)
Crown St. *Eastb* —3F **17**
Croxden Way. *Eastb* —2F **13**
Crunden Rd. *Eastb* —3E **17**
Cuckmere Dri. *Sto X* —6A **8**
Cuckmere Ho. *Eastb*
—4H **17** (1C **22**)

Cuckmere Wlk. *Eastb* —4F **13**
Cuckoo Trail. *Hail* —4C **2**
(in two parts)
Cuckoo Trail. *Pol* —3C **6**
Cullenswood Ct. *Eastb* —6B **22**
Culver Clo. *Eastb* —1B **14**
Cumbria Ct. *Eastb* —2C **14**
Cunningham Dri. *Eastb* —6E **15**

Dacre Pk. *Hail* —2F **5**
Dacre Rd. *Eastb* —4E **17**
Dale Ct. *Eastb* —6G **17** (6B **22**)
Dallaway Dri. *Sto X* —6B **8**
Dallington Rd. *Eastb* —4H **13**
Dalton Rd. *Eastb* —1G **21**
Danum Clo. *Hail* —4E **3**
Darley Rd. *Eastb* —1F **21**
Darrick Ct. *Eastb* —6E **23**
Darwell Dri. *Sto X* —6A **8**
David Heights. *Eastb* —2G **17**
Dean Wood Clo. *Eastb* —1A **14**
Decoy Dri. *Eastb* —5F **13**
Decoy Roundabout. *Eastb*
—5F **13**
Deer Paddock La. Hail —2E **5**
(off Station Rd.)
Delamere Ct. *Eastb* —3D **22**
Delavall Wlk. *Eastb* —1F **19**
Dene Clo. *E Dean* —2B **20**
Dene Ct. *Eastb* —5H **17** (3D **22**)
Dene Dri. *Eastb* —4E **13**
Deneside. *E Dean* —2B **20**
Dene, The. *Eastb* —2C **12**
Den Hill. *Eastb* —3C **16**
Denstone Ho. *Eastb*
—5H **17** (4D **22**)
Denton Rd. *Eastb*
—1F **21** (6A **22**)
Dentons, The. *Eastb* —1F **21**
De Roos Rd. *Eastb* —3G **17**
Derry Ct. *Eastb* —4D **14**
Derwent Clo. *Hail* —6C **2**
Derwent Rd. *Eastb* —1G **21**
Desmond Rd. *Eastb* —2D **18**
Devonshire Lodge. Eastb
(off Roselands Av.) —2C **18**
Devonshire Pl. *Eastb*
—5A **18** (3F **23**)
De Walden Ct. *Eastb*
—6G **17** (6A **22**)
De Walden M. *Eastb* —1G **21**
Dickens Way. *Eastb* —2E **15**
Dillingburgh Rd. *Eastb* —3E **17**
Diplock Clo. *Pol* —5B **6**
Diplocks, The. *Hail* —2C **4**
Diplocks Wlk. *Hail* —1C **4**
Diplocks Way. *Hail* —2C **4**
Ditchling Clo. *Eastb* —1H **13**
Ditchling Way. *Hail* —3D **4**
Dittons Grange. *Eastb*
—4G **17** (2B **22**)
Dittons Rd. *Eastb*
—4G **17** (2B **22**)
Dittons Rd. *Pol & Sto X* —5F **7**
Dolphin Ct. *Eastb* —2G **21**
Donegal Ct. Eastb —4D **14**
(off Pembury Rd.)
Dorset Ct. *Eastb* —1G **23**
Douglas Clo. *Hail* —5D **2**
Dovedale Gdns. *Eastb* —3H **13**
Dover Rd. *Pol* —4D **6**
Downlands Way. *E Dean*
—2B **20**
Downs Av. *Eastb* —1D **16**
Downside Clo. *Eastb* —4E **17**
Downsmeade. *Eastb*
—4G **17** (1B **22**)

Hailsham Rd. *Hers* —4F **3**
Hailsham Rd. *Pol* —4B **6**
Hailsham Rd. *Sto X* —2G **7**
Halland Clo. *Eastb* —5F **13**
Halley Pk. *Hail* —2F **5**
Halton Rd. *Eastb* —3C **18**
Hamble Rd. *Sto X* —6H **7**
Hambleton Clo. *Eastb* —2D **14**
Hamelsham Ct. *Hail* —1C **4**
Hamilton Ho. *Eastb*
—3G **17** (1B **22**)
Hamlands La. *Eastb* —2D **12**
Hammonds Dri. *Eastb* —6C **14**
Hampden Av. *Eastb* —4H **13**
Hampden Ct. *Eastb* —5E **23**
Hampden Pk. *Eastb* —1G **17**
Hampden Pk. Dri. *Eastb*
—5F **13**
Hampden Pk. Ind. Est. *Eastb*
—5H **13**
Hampden Pk. Relief Rd. *Eastb*
—1G **17**
Hampden Retail Pk. *Eastb*
—4H **13**
Hampden Ter. *Eastb* —1H **23**
Hampshire Ct. *Eastb* —4E **15**
Hamsey Clo. *Eastb* —1D **16**
Ham Shaw La. *Eastb* —5H **13**
Hankham Hall Rd. *Hank &*
W'ham —3B **8**
Hankham Rd. *Hank* —5B **8**
Hankham St. *Hank* —4B **8**
Hanover Ct. *Eastb* —2F **17**
Hanover Rd. *Eastb* —3C **18**
Harding Av. *Eastb* —1B **18**
Hardwick Rd. *Eastb*
—5A **18** (3E **23**)
Hardy Dri. *Eastb* —1F **19**
Harebeating Clo. *Hail* —5E **3**
Harebeating Cres. *Hail* —5E **3**
Harebeating Dri. *Hail* —4D **2**
Harebeating Gdns. *Hail* —5E **3**
Harebeating La. *Hail* —5E **3**
Harebell Clo. *Eastb* —2C **14**
Harford Battersby Ho. *Eastb*
—3F **23**
Hargreaves Rd. *Eastb* —4A **14**
Harmers Hay Rd. *Hail* —5D **2**
Harold Clo. *Pev B* —3D **10**
Harold Dri. *Eastb* —5E **15**
Harris Ct. *Eastb* —4A **18** (2F **23**)
Hartfield La. *Eastb*
—3H **17** (1D **22**)
Hartfield Rd. *Eastb*
—4H **17** (1C **22**)
Hartington Mans. *Eastb* —4F **23**
Hartington Pl. *Eastb*
—5A **18** (3F **23**)
Harwood Clo. *Eastb* —6E **15**
Hassocks Clo. *Eastb* —1H **13**
Hastings Rd. *Pol* —4D **6**
Havelock Rd. *Eastb* —3B **18**
Haven Clo. *Eastb* —2D **12**
Haven Clo. *Pev B* —3C **10**
Hawkhurst Clo. *Eastb* —3D **14**
Hawkins Way. *Hail* —1D **4**
Hawksbridge Clo. *Eastb*
—2D **12**
Hawks Farm Clo. *Hail* —5D **2**
Hawks Rd. *Hail* —6D **2**
Hawkstown Clo. *Hail* —4D **2**
Hawks Town Cres. *Hail* —5D **2**
Hawkstown Gdns. *Hail* —4D **2**
Hawkstown View. *Hail* —4D **2**
Hawkswood Dri. *Hail* —4E **3**
Hawkswood Rd. *Hail* —4D **2**
Hawthorn Rd. *Eastb* —5C **14**
Hawthorns, The. *Hail* —2C **4**

Hawthylands Cres. *Hail* —5D **3**
Hawthylands Dri. *Hail* —5D **2**
Hawthylands Rd. *Hail* —5D **2**
Hayland Grn. *Hail* —6E **3**
Haystoun Clo. *Eastb* —3E **13**
Haystoun Pk. *Eastb* —3E **13**
Hazel Gro. *Eastb* —2C **12**
Hazelwood Av. *Eastb* —2F **13**
Heather Clo. *Eastb* —2B **14**
Helvellyn Dri. *Eastb* —1C **14**
Hempstead La. *Hail* —2A **4**
Hendy Av. *Eastb* —2C **18**
Henfield Rd. *Eastb* —3G **13**
Hengist Clo. *Eastb* —5F **15**
Henleaze. *Eastb*
—4G **17** (1B **22**)
Hereford Ct. *Eastb* —4E **15**
Hereward Rd. *Eastb* —4F **15**
Heron Clo. *Eastb* —3C **14**
Heron Ridge. *Pol* —5D **6**
Hever Clo. *Eastb* —3D **14**
Hickling Clo. *Eastb* —1B **14**
Hide Hollow. *Eastb* —2D **14**
Hide Hollow Roundabout. *Eastb*
—2C **14**
High Clo. *E Dean* —1C **20**
Highcombe. *Eastb* —2F **21**
Highfield Ind. Est. *Eastb*
—4A **14**
Highfield Link. *Eastb* —5A **14**
Highland Lodge. *Eastb* —3H **17**
Highmead Mnr. *Eastb* —1G **21**
High St. Eastbourne, *Eastb*
—4F **17** (1A **22**)
High St. Hailsham, *Hail* —1D **4**
High St. Pevensey, *Pev* —5H **9**
High St. Polegate, *Pol* —5C **6**
High St. Westham, *W'ham*
—5F **9**
High Trees. *Eastb* —3H **17**
Highview Ct. *Eastb*
—6H **17** (6D **22**)
Hilary Clo. *Pol* —6B **6**
Hill Ct. *Eastb* —6D **22**
Hill Gdns. *Hail* —5B **2**
Hill Rd. *Eastb* —2C **16**
Hillside. *E Dean* —2B **20**
Hoad Rd. *Eastb* —3B **18**
Hobney Ri. *W'ham* —6F **9**
Hockington La. *Eastb* —4D **12**
Hodcombe Clo. *Eastb* —1B **14**
Hogarth Rd. *Eastb* —4D **14**
Holbrook Clo. *Eastb* —1G **21**
Hollamby Pk. *Hail* —2F **5**
Holly Clo. *Hail* —3D **4**
Holly Pl. *Eastb* —2G **13**
Holt, The. *Hail* —3C **4**
Holyhead Clo. *Eastb* —6C **2**
Holywell Clo. *Eastb* —2G **21**
Holywell Rd. *Eastb* —2G **21**
Holywell Wlk. Hail —2D **4**
(off Lindfield Dri.)
Homegate Ho. *Eastb* —1D **22**
Homedale Ho. *Eastb* —1G **22**
Homewood Clo. *Eastb* —1B **18**
Honeycrag Clo. *Pol* —4B **6**
Honeysuckle Clo. *Eastb*
—2B **14**
Honeysuckle Clo. *Hail* —4D **4**
Honeyway Clo. *Pol* —2B **12**
Hood Clo. *Eastb* —6E **15**
Hoo Gdns. *Eastb* —4D **12**
Horning Clo. *Eastb* —1B **14**
Horsa Clo. *Eastb* —5F **15**
Horsye Rd. *Eastb* —6B **14**
Howard Clo. *Hail* —3F **5**
Howard Ho. *Eastb*
—6A **18** (5F **23**)

Howard Sq. *Eastb*
—5A **18** (4F **23**)
Howlett Dri. *Hail* —5D **2**
Howletts Clo. *Eastb* —4H **13**
Hudson Clo. *Eastb* —6G **15**
Hudson Ct. *Eastb* —1C **18**
(off Churchdale Rd.)
Huggett's La. *Eastb* —3D **12**
Hunloke Av. *Eastb* —1B **18**
Hurst La. *Eastb* —3F **17**
Hurst Rd. *Eastb* —2F **17**
Hyde Gdns. *Eastb*
—5A **18** (3E **23**)
Hyde Rd. *Eastb*
—5H **17** (3D **22**)
Hyde Tynings Clo. *Eastb*
—1E **21**
Hydneye St. *Eastb* —2C **18**
Hydneye, The. *Eastb* —4H **13**
Hyperion Av. *Pol* —5A **6**
Hythe Clo. *Pol* —4E **7**

Iden St. *Eastb* —3A **14**
Ifield Mill Clo. *Pev* —6B **8**
Ilex Grn. *Hail* —6D **2**
Ingrams Way. *Hail* —4C **4**
Innings Dri. *Pev B* —5A **10**
Ivy La. *Eastb* —3H **17**
Ivy Ter. *Eastb* —4H **17** (2D **22**)

Jack O'Dandy Clo. *Eastb*
—6E **13**
Jamaica Way. *Eastb* —5F **15**
Jasmine Grn. *Hail* —6D **2**
Jay Clo. *Eastb* —3C **14**
Jellicoe Clo. *Eastb* —1F **19**
Jephson Clo. *Eastb*
—1H **21** (6C **22**)
Jerome Clo. *Eastb* —3E **15**
Jervis Av. *Eastb* —1E **19**
Jevington Gdns. *Eastb*
—6H **17** (6D **22**)
Jevington Ho. Eastb —3F **17**
(off Upperton Rd.)
Jevington Rd. *Pol* —3A **12**
John Hughes Ct. *Pol* —6C **6**
Jordans La. *Eastb* —2F **13**
Jordans La. E. *Eastb* —2F **13**
Jordans La. W. *Eastb* —2E **13**
Junction Rd. *Eastb*
—4A **18** (2E **23**)
Junction St. *Pol* —5D **6**

Keats Wlk. *Eastb* —2E **15**
(off Priory Rd.)
Keith Wlk. *Eastb* —1F **19**
Kennett Clo. *Sto X* —6H **7**
Kent Ct. *Eastb* —1D **16**
Kent Ho. *Eastb* —1G **21**
Kenton Ct. *Eastb* —6E **23**
Kepplestone. *Eastb* —1G **21**
Kerrara Ter. *Eastb* —2B **18**
Kerry Ct. *Eastb* —4D **14**
Keymer Clo. *Eastb* —4E **15**
Keymer Ho. *Eastb* —1A **22**
Kilburn Ter. *Eastb*
—4A **18** (1E **23**)
Kildare Ct. *Eastb* —4E **17**
Kilda St. *Eastb* —3B **18**
Kilpatrick Clo. *Eastb* —2D **14**
Kinfauns Av. *Eastb* —1B **18**
King Edwards Pde. *Eastb*
—2G **18** (6E **23**)
Kingfisher Dri. *Eastb* —3C **14**
King's Av. *Eastb* —2G **17**

Kings Clo. *Eastb* —2G **17**
King's Dri. *Eastb* —5E **13**
Kingsford. *Eastb* —6D **14**
Kingsmere Way. *Eastb* —5E **15**
Kingston Ho. *Eastb*
—3H **17** (1C **22**)
Kingston Rd. *Eastb* —3H **13**
Kinross Ct. *Eastb* —3A **18**
Kipling Wlk. *Eastb* —3E **15**
Kirkstall Clo. *Eastb* —2G **13**
Kirk Way. *Eastb* —2D **16**
Knights Garden. *Hail* —3D **4**
Knoll Cres. *Eastb* —3A **14**
Knoll Rd. *Eastb* —3A **14**

Laburnum Grn. *Hail* —6D **2**
Laburnum Wlk. *Eastb* —2F **13**
Labyrinth, The. *Eastb* —2E **23**
Lakelands Clo. *Eastb* —4A **14**
Lakeside Ct. *Eastb* —4A **14**
Laleham Clo. *Eastb* —3G **17**
Laleham Ct. *Eastb* —3G **17**
Lambert Rd. *Eastb* —2E **15**
Lambourn Av. *Sto X* —6A **8**
Lamont Ct. *Eastb* —6E **23**
Lanark Ct. *Eastb* —1D **16**
Lancaster Ct. *Eastb* —1H **23**
Lancing Way. *Pol* —1B **12**
Langdale Clo. *Eastb* —1C **14**
Langney Grn. *Eastb* —5E **15**
Langney Ri. *Eastb* —2C **14**
(in two parts)
Langney Rd. *Eastb*
—4A **18** (2F **23**)
Langney Roundabout. *Eastb*
—5E **15**
Langney Shopping Cen. *Eastb*
—3C **14**
Lansdowne Ct. *Eastb* —5E **23**
Lansdowne Cres. *Hail* —5C **2**
Lansdowne Dri. *Hail* —4C **2**
Lansdowne Gdns. *Hail* —5D **2**
Lansdowne Rd. *Hail* —5D **2**
Lansdowne Way. *Hail* —4C **2**
Lapwing Clo. *Eastb* —3C **14**
Larch Gdns. *Eastb* —2F **13**
Larkspur Dri. *Eastb* —1A **14**
La Ronde Ct. *Eastb* —3F **23**
Lascelles Mans. *Eastb* —5F **23**
Lascelles Ter. *Eastb*
—6A **18** (5F **23**)
Latimer Ct. Eastb —3C **18**
(off Latimer Rd.)
Latimer Rd. *Eastb*
—3C **18** (1H **23**)
Laughton Clo. *Eastb* —1A **14**
Laura Hoy Wlk. *Eastb*
—4F **17** (2A **22**)
Lavant Rd. *Sto X* —6B **8**
Lavender Clo. *Eastb* —2B **14**
Lavender Clo. *Hail* —6B **2**
Lawns Av. *Eastb*
—3F **17** (1A **22**)
Lawns, The. *Eastb* —4D **12**
(nr. Hoo Gdns.)
Lawns, The. *Eastb* —2C **18**
(nr. Roselands Av.)
Lawns, The. *Will* —3D **12**
Lawrence Clo. *Eastb* —4D **14**
Leaf Hall Rd. *Eastb*
—4B **18** (1H **23**)
Leaf Rd. *Eastb* —4A **18** (1F **23**)
Lea Ho. *Eastb* —3G **17**
Leahurst. *Eastb* —1H **21** (6B **22**)
Leamland Wlk. *Hail* —2D **4**
(off Lindfield Dri.)
Le Brun Rd. *Eastb* —2G **17**

Leeds Av. *Eastb* —5D **14**
Leeward Quay. *Eastb* —5F **15**
Leicester Ct. *Eastb* —3B **18**
  (off Leslie St.)
Lennox Clo. *Eastb* —2D **16**
Lepeland. *Hail* —6C **2**
Leslie St. *Eastb* —3B **18**
Letheren Pl. *Eastb* —4F **17**
Le Vett Av. *Pol* —4E **7**
Le Vett Clo. *Pol* —5E **7**
Le Vett Rd. *Pol* —5E **7**
Le Vett Way. *Pol* —5E **7**
Lewes Rd. *Eastb* —2H **17**
Lewes Rd. *Pol* —5A **6**
Leyland Rd. *Pev B* —5B **10**
Lilac Clo. *Eastb* —3F **13**
Limes, The. *Eastb*
  —3G **17** (1B **22**)
Limetree Av. *Eastb* —2F **13**
Lincoln Clo. *Eastb* —1E **21**
Lincoln Ct. *Eastb* —1D **16**
Linden Clo. *Eastb* —2G **13**
Linden Gro. *Amb* —4E **3**
Linden Rd. *Pev* —6A **8**
Lindfield Dri. *Hail* —2D **4**
Lindfield Rd. *Eastb* —3F **13**
Lindsay Clo. *Eastb* —5E **17**
Link Rd. *Eastb* —6F **17** (6A **22**)
Linkswood. *Eastb*
  —5G **17** (3A **22**)
Link, The. *E Dean* —1C **20**
Linkway. *Eastb* —6D **12**
Linkway, The. *W'ham* —5E **9**
Linnet Clo. *Eastb* —3C **14**
Linosa Ct. *Eastb* —1H **23**
Linton Clo. *E Dean* —2B **20**
Lion Hill. *Sto X* —6B **8**
Lion La. *Eastb* —4B **18** (2H **23**)
Lismore Rd. *Eastb*
  —5A **18** (3F **23**)
Lister Rd. *Eastb* —4A **14**
Littlecote. *Eastb*
  —6H **17** (5C **22**)
Lodge Av. *Eastb* —3E **13**
Lodge, The. *Eastb* —4E **23**
London Ho. *Eastb* —3E **23**
London Rd. *Hail* —4C **2**
Long Acre Clo. *Eastb* —2F **17**
Longford Ct. *Eastb* —3D **14**
Longland Rd. *Eastb* —3D **16**
Longstone Rd. *Eastb*
  —4A **18** (2F **23**)
Lordslaine Clo. *Eastb* —1E **21**
Lothian Ct. *Eastb* —3H **13**
Lottbridge Drove. *Eastb*
  —3H **13**
Lottbridge Roundabout. *Eastb*
  —5A **14**
Love La. *Eastb* —4F **17** (2A **22**)
Lower Rd. *Eastb* —3F **17**
Lower St. *E Dean* —3B **20**
Lowlands, The. *Hail* —6C **2**
Lowther Clo. *Eastb* —2D **14**
Loxwood Clo. *Eastb* —5E **13**
Lullington Clo. *Eastb* —6E **13**
Lullington Ho. *Eastb* —3G **17**
Lundy Wlk. *Hail* —4B **2**
Lushington La. *Eastb*
  —5A **18** (3E **23**)
Lushington Rd. *Eastb*
  —5A **18** (3E **23**)
Luton Clo. *Eastb* —1E **17**
Lydd Clo. *Eastb* —3D **14**
Lynholm Rd. *Pol* —5E **7**

Macmillan Dri. *Eastb* —2E **17**
Magdalen Clo. *Eastb* —2C **14**

Magellan Way. *Eastb* —1F **19**
Magnolia Dri. *Eastb* —3F **13**
Magnolia Wlk. *Eastb* —3F **13**
Magpie Rd. *Eastb* —2C **14**
Malcolm Gdns. *Pol* —4C **6**
Mallard Clo. *Eastb* —4H **13**
Malthouse Cotts. *Eastb* —4D **12**
  (off Wish Hill)
Malvern Clo. *Eastb* —2F **13**
Manifold Rd. *Eastb* —3B **18**
Manor Clo. *Eastb* —3C **12**
Manor Pk. Clo. *Hail* —4C **2**
Manor Pk. Rd. *Hail* —4C **2**
Manor Rd. *Eastb* —3A **14**
Manor Way. *Eastb* —5D **12**
Manor Way. *Pol* —5C **6**
Manton Ct. *Eastb* —5D **14**
Manvers Rd. *Eastb* —4D **16**
Maple Ct. *Hail* —1C **4**
Maplehurst Rd. *Eastb* —3F **13**
Mapleleaf Gdns. *Pol* —3C **6**
Maple Rd. *Eastb* —6D **14**
Marcia Clo. *Eastb* —5C **12**
Maresfield Dri. *Pev B* —3C **10**
Marina Wlk. *Eastb* —5E **15**
Marine Av. *Pev B* —3D **10**
Marine Clo. *Pev B* —3D **10**
Marine Pde. *Eastb*
  —5B **18** (3H **23**)
Marine Rd. *Eastb*
  —4B **18** (1H **23**)
Marine Rd. *Pev B* —4B **10**
Marine Ter. *Pev B* —4B **10**
Market Pl. *Hail* —2E **5**
Market Sq. *Hail* —2E **5**
  (off Market St.)
Market St. *Hail* —2E **5**
Mark La. *Eastb* —5A **18** (3E **23**)
Marlborough Clo. *Eastb*
  —2D **14**
Marlow Av. *Eastb* —1B **18**
Marsden Rd. *Eastb* —4E **15**
Marshall Ct. *Eastb* —4F **13**
Marshall Rd. *Eastb* —5H **13**
Marshall Roundabout. *Eastb*
  —5A **14**
Marshfoot La. *Hail* —1E **5**
Martello Beach Cvn. Pk. *Pev*
  —6A **10**
Martello Ct. *Pev* —6A **10**
Martello Rd. *Eastb* —1D **18**
Martello Roundabout. *Eastb*
  —4G **15**
Martin Ct. *Eastb* —4F **13**
Martlet Ho. *Eastb* —2G **23**
Maryan St. *Hail* —1D **4**
Matlock Rd. *Eastb* —1G **21**
Maxfield Clo. *Eastb* —2D **16**
Mayfair Clo. *Pol* —1B **12**
Mayfair Ho. *Eastb*
  —5A **18** (3E **23**)
Mayfield Pl. *Eastb* —3A **18**
Mayo Ct. *Eastb* —4D **14**
  (off Pembury Rd.)
Maywood Av. *Eastb* —3F **13**
Meachants Ct. *Eastb* —3D **12**
Meachants La. *Eastb* —3C **12**
Meadhurst. *Eastb* —5B **22**
Meadow Clo. *Hail* —6D **2**
Meadowlands Av. *Eastb*
  —3F **13**
Meadow Rd. *Hail* —3C **4**
Meadows Rd. *Eastb* —3D **12**
Meads Brow. *Eastb* —1F **21**
Meads Ct. *Eastb*
  —6G **17** (5B **22**)
Meads Rd. *Eastb*
  —1G **21** (6A **22**)

Meads Roundabout. *Eastb*
  —1G **21** (6A **22**)
Meads St. *Eastb* —1G **21**
Meadsway. *Eastb* —1G **21**
Medina Dri. *Sto X* —6B **8**
Medway. *Hail* —5C **2**
Medway La. *Sto X* —6A **8**
Melbourne Rd. *Eastb*
  —4B **18** (1G **23**)
Melrose Clo. *Hail* —1C **4**
Melvill La. *Eastb* —5D **12**
Mendip Av. *Eastb* —2C **14**
Meon Clo. *Pev* —6A **8**
Merewood Ct. *Eastb* —3G **17**
Merlin Ct. *Hail* —2G **5**
Merlswood. *Eastb*
  —6G **17** (5B **22**)
Merlynn. *Eastb* —4F **23**
Metropole Ct. *Eastb* —2H **23**
Mewett's Ct. *Eastb* —2D **12**
Michel Clo. *E Dean* —2C **20**
Michel Dene Clo. *E Dean*
  —2C **20**
Michel Dene Rd. *E Dean*
  —2B **20**
Michel Dene Rd. *Fris* —1C **20**
Michel Gro. *Eastb*
  —4G **17** (1A **22**)
Michel Gro. Ho. *Eastb*
  —4G **17** (1B **22**)
Michelham Clo. *Eastb* —1A **14**
Middleham Clo. *Eastb* —1C **14**
Middlesex Ct. *Eastb* —3B **18**
  (off Leslie St.)
Middleton Dri. *Eastb* —6E **15**
Midhurst Rd. *Eastb* —3H **13**
Milchester Ho. *Eastb* —1G **21**
  (off Buxton Rd.)
Milfoil Dri. *Eastb* —1B **14**
Milland Rd. *Hail* —6D **2**
Millbrook Gdns. *Eastb* —1D **16**
Mill Clo. *Fris* —2A **20**
Mill Clo. *Pol* —1B **12**
Millers Ri. *Hail* —3C **4**
Millfield Ct. *Eastb*
  —4G **17** (1B **22**)
Millfields Ct. *Pol* —4C **6**
Mill Gap Rd. *Eastb* —3H **17**
Mill La. *Hell* —2C **2**
Millrace, The. *Pol* —1B **12**
Mill Rd. *Eastb* —2F **17**
Mill Rd. *Hail* —2E **5**
Millstream Gdns. *Pol* —1B **12**
Mill View Clo. *W'ham* —5D **8**
Millward Rd. *Pev B* —6A **10**
Mill Way. *Pol* —2A **12**
Milnthorpe Gdns. *Eastb* —1G **21**
Milnthorpe Rd. *Eastb* —1G **21**
Milton Cres. *Eastb* —3E **17**
Milton Rd. *Eastb* —2E **17**
Milton St. *Hank* —5A **8**
Mimosa Clo. *Pol* —3C **6**
Mimram Rd. *Pev* —6A **8**
Minster Clo. *Pol* —4C **6**
Mirasol. *Eastb* —6C **22**
Moat Cft. Ct. *Eastb*
  —4G **17** (1A **22**)
Moat Cft. Rd. *Eastb*
  —4G **17** (1A **22**)
Moat Ho. *Eastb*
  —4G **17** (1A **22**)
Monarch Gdns. *Eastb* —4F **15**
Monarch Ho. *Eastb* —1E **19**
Mona Rd. *Eastb* —3B **18**
Mona St. *Eastb* —2B **18**
Monceux Rd. *Eastb* —3E **17**
Monk Sherborne Ho. *Eastb*
  —5C **22**

Montague Way. *W'ham* —6F **9**
Montfort Clo. *W'ham* —5F **9**
Montfort Rd. *W'ham* —5F **9**
Moore Pk. *Hail* —2F **5**
Moorings, The. *Eastb* —1G **21**
  (off St John's Rd.)
Moray Wlk. *Hail* —5C **2**
Mortain Pk. *Hail* —2F **5**
Mortain Rd. *W'ham* —5F **9**
Mortimer Gdns. *Pol* —1B **12**
Mortimer Rd. *Eastb* —1A **18**
Moss Ho. *Eastb*
  —5H **17** (3D **22**)
Motcombe La. *Eastb* —3F **17**
Motcombe Rd. *Eastb* —3F **17**
Mountain Ash Clo. *Hail* —1C **4**
Mountbatten Dri. *Eastb* —6E **15**
Mountfield Rd. *Eastb* —4H **13**
Mountfield Roundabout. *Eastb*
  —4H **13**
Mountney Bri. Bus. Pk. *W'ham*
  —1F **15**
Mountney Dri. *Pev B* —3D **10**
Mountney Rd. *Eastb* —3E **17**
Mount Rd. *Eastb* —1H **21**
Mount, The. *Eastb*
  —6G **17** (6B **22**)
Mount, The. *Hail* —3E **5**
Mt. View Ter. *Hail* —3E **5**
Mowbray Ct. *Eastb* —5F **23**
Moy Av. *Eastb* —2B **18**
Mulberry Clo. *Eastb* —2G **13**
Myrtle Rd. *Eastb* —1D **18**

Naomi Clo. *Eastb*
  —6G **17** (6B **22**)
Nelson Dri. *Eastb* —1E **19**
Netherfield Av. *Eastb* —3F **15**
Nevill Av. *Eastb* —4G **13**
Neville Rd. *Eastb* —3B **18**
New Barn Clo. *Hail* —3E **5**
New College Clo. *Eastb* —2C **14**
New Derby Ho. *Eastb* —6D **14**
Newick Rd. *Eastb* —1E **17**
New Pl. *Eastb* —4F **17**
New Rd. *Eastb* —3B **18** (1G **23**)
  (in two parts)
New Rd. *Hell* —3D **2**
New Rd. *Pol* —5D **6**
Newton Pk. *Hail* —2F **5**
New Upperton Rd. *Eastb*
  —3G **17** (1A **22**)
Nicholson Ct. *Eastb* —4E **15**
Nightingale La. *Eastb* —3C **14**
Nodes La. *Hail* —3H **3**
Norfolk Ct. *Eastb* —3C **18**
  (off Redoubt Rd.)
Norman Rd. *Pev B* —5B **10**
North Av. *Eastb* —2D **16**
Northbourne Rd. *Eastb* —1B **18**
North Clo. *Pol* —4D **6**
Northern Av. *Pol* —4D **6**
Northfield. *Pol* —6B **6**
N. Heath La. *Hail* —5E **3**
Northiam Rd. *Eastb* —3E **17**
North Rd. *Pev B* —5B **10**
North St. *Eastb*
  —5B **18** (2G **23**)
North St. *Hail* —1D **4**
North St. *Hell* —3A **2**
Northumberland Ct. *Eastb*
  —3A **14**
Norway Rd. *Eastb* —1D **18**
Nursery Clo. *Hail* —1E **5**
Nursery Clo. *Pol* —5D **6**
Nursery Path. *Hail* —3D **4**
Nutbourne Clo. *Eastb* —3E **15**

Nuthatch Rd. *Eastb* —3C **14**
Nutley Mill Rd. *Sto X* —6B **8**

Oaklands. *W'ham* —5D **8**
Oaklands Clo. *Pol* —5D **6**
Oaklands Way. *Hail* —3C **4**
Oakleaf Ct. *Pol* —4C **6**
Oakleaf Dri. *Pol* —4C **6**
Oakley Down. *Eastb*
—6G **17** (6B **22**)
Oak Tree La. *Eastb* —1C **14**
Oak Tree Way. *Hail* —5E **3**
Observatory Vw. *Hail* —2F **5**
Ocklynge Av. *Eastb* —3F **17**
Ocklynge Rd. *Eastb*
—3F **17** (1A **22**)
Offham Clo. *Eastb* —1H **13**
Okehurst Rd. *Eastb* —4E **17**
Old Barn Clo. *Eastb* —4D **12**
Old Camp Rd. *Eastb* —5E **17**
Old Drive. *Pol* —5B **6**
Old Drove. *Eastb* —2C **14**
Oldfield Av. *Eastb* —2C **12**
Oldfield Cres. *Hail* —6D **2**
Oldfield Rd. *Eastb* —1C **12**
Old Mansion Clo. *Eastb* —5C **12**
Old Mill Clo. *Hail* —4C **2**
Old Mill La. *Pol* —2A **12**
Old Motcombe M. *Eastb*
—3F **17**
Old Orchard Pl. *Hail* —2D **4**
Old Orchard Rd. *Eastb*
—5H **17** (3C **22**)
Old Rd. *Mag D* —4H **3**
Old Swan La. *Hail* —4F **5**
Old Willingdon Rd. *Fris* —2A **20**
Old Wish Rd. *Eastb*
—6H **17** (5D **22**)
Ollier Ct. *Eastb* —6H **17** (5D **22**)
Orchard Pde. *Eastb* —2C **12**
Orchid Clo. *Eastb* —2B **14**
Orion Clo. *Hail* —2F **5**
Orkney Ct. *Eastb* —1D **16**
Orwell Clo. *Pev* —6B **8**
Osbourne Rd. *Eastb* —3D **16**
Otham Ct. La. *Pol* —3C **6**
Otham Pk. *Hail* —2F **5**
Otham Rd. *Eastb* —3A **14**
Otteham Clo. *Pol* —5D **6**
Oulton Clo. *Eastb* —2B **14**
Outlook, The. *Fris* —2A **20**
Oxendean Gdns. *Eastb* —1D **12**
Oxford Rd. *Eastb* —3B **18**

Paddock Gdns. *Pol* —1B **12**
Paddocks, The. *Hail* —5C **2**
Paddock, The. *Eastb* —3H **13**
Pagham Clo. *Eastb* —1B **14**
Palgrave Ho. *Eastb* —1H **23**
Palliser Clo. *Eastb* —1E **19**
Palma Clo. *Pol* —4C **6**
Parade, The. *Blnds* —3D **10**
Parade, The. *Pev B* —4B **10**
Paradise Clo. *Eastb* —5F **17**
Paradise Dri. *Eastb*
—6E **17** (3A **22**)
Paragon, The. *Eastb* —2B **12**
Park Av. *Eastb* —6E **13**
Park Clo. *Eastb* —4F **17** (2A **22**)
Park Clo. *Hail* —3D **4**
Park Cft. *Pol* —1C **12**
Parker Clo. *Eastb* —2G **17**
Parkfield Av. *Eastb* —4F **13**
Park Ga. *Amb* —4F **3**
Park Gates. *Eastb*
—5A **18** (4F **23**)

Parkholme. *Eastb* —6B **22**
Park Ho. *Eastb* —4F **23**
(nr. Burlington Pl.)
Park Ho. *Eastb* —5A **18** (4E **23**)
(nr. College Rd.)
Park La. *Eastb* —5E **13**
Park Lodge. *Eastb* —4F **23**
Park Lodge. *Eastb*
—5A **18** (4E **23**)
(off Blackwater Rd.)
Park Rd. *Hell* —4D **2**
Parkway. *Eastb* —5C **12**
Parry Clo. *Eastb* —2E **15**
Parsonage Rd. *Eastb* —3F **17**
Pashley Ct. *Eastb* —5E **17**
Pashley Rd. *Eastb* —5D **16**
Patcham Mill Rd. *Sto X* —6B **8**
Paul Clo. *Hail* —4C **2**
Pauling Ho. *Eastb* —4E **23**
Peakdean Clo. *Fris* —1B **20**
Peakdean La. *Fris* —1C **20**
Pearl Ct. *Eastb* —3F **23**
Pebble Rd. *Pev B* —4C **10**
Peelings La. *W'ham* —6B **8**
Pelham Clo. *W'ham* —6F **9**
Pelham Cres. *Hail* —3E **5**
Pembroke Clo. *Amb* —4E **3**
Pembroke Ho. *Eastb* —1C **22**
Pembroke Ho. *Eastb*
—4H **17** (2C **22**)
(off Upperton Rd.)
Pembury Rd. *Eastb* —4D **14**
Penhale Rd. *Eastb* —2D **18**
Penhurst Clo. *Eastb* —4A **14**
Pennine Way. *Eastb* —2C **14**
Penrith Way. *Eastb* —1C **14**
Pensford Dri. *Eastb* —2D **14**
Pentland Clo. *Eastb* —2D **14**
Peppercombe Rd. *Eastb*
—3D **16**
Pepys Wlk. *Eastb* —3E **15**
(off Rising, The)
Percival Cres. *Eastb* —2H **13**
Percival Rd. *Eastb* —2H **13**
Perth Ct. *Eastb* —3A **18**
Petworth Pl. *Eastb* —3G **13**
Pevensey Bay Rd. *Eastb*
—5E **15**
Pevensey By-Pass. *Pev* —5H **7**
Pevensey Ct. *Pev B* —4B **10**
Pevensey Pk. Rd. *W'ham* —5F **9**
Pevensey Rd. *Eastb*
—4A **18** (3F **23**)
Pevensey Rd. *Pol* —5D **6**
Peyton Clo. *Eastb* —6F **15**
Phoenix Clo. *Hail* —2F **5**
Phoenix Ct. *Eastb* —1H **23**
Piltdown Way. *Eastb* —1A **14**
Pine Way. *Hail* —2C **4**
Pinewood Clo. *Eastb* —3F **13**
Pitreavie Dri. *Hail* —1C **4**
Plover Clo. *Eastb* —3C **14**
Plumpton Clo. *Eastb* —1A **14**
Plymouth Clo. *Eastb* —5F **15**
Pocock's Rd. *Eastb* —2F **17**
Polegate By-Pass. *Pol* —2B **6**
Polegate Rd. *Hail* —4C **4**
Poplar Wlk. *Eastb* —2F **13**
Porters Way. *Pol* —5C **6**
Portland Clo. *Hail* —6C **2**
Portlands, The. *Eastb* —6F **15**
Port Rd. *Eastb* —4A **14**
Portsdown Way. *Eastb* —3D **12**
Potts Marsh Ind. Est. *W'ham*
—1F **15**
Pound Clo. *Eastb* —1F **19**
Prideaux Ct. *Eastb* —2H **17**
Prideaux Rd. *Eastb* —2G **17**

Primrose Clo. *Eastb* —2B **14**
Princes Rd. *Eastb* —1E **19**
Prince William Pde. *Eastb*
—1E **19**
Priory Clo. *Pev B* —4B **10**
Priory Ct. *Eastb* —5C **22**
Priory Heights. *Eastb* —2C **16**
Priory La. *Eastb* —2E **15**
Priory Orchard. *Eastb* —4E **15**
Priory Rd. *Eastb* —2E **15**
Priory Roundabout. *Eastb*
—2E **15**
Promenade. *Eastb*
—1H **21** (6E **23**)
Promenade, The. *Pev B* —5B **10**
Prospect Gdns. *Eastb* —3F **17**
Pulborough Av. *Eastb* —4G **13**
Purbeck Clo. *Eastb* —2C **14**

Quadrant, The. *Eastb* —3G **17**
Quantock Clo. *Eastb* —2D **14**
Quebec Clo. *Eastb* —6F **15**
Queens Ct. *Eastb* —6D **14**
Queen's Cres. *Eastb* —6D **14**
Queen's Gdns. *Eastb*
—4B **18** (2H **23**)
Queen's Rd. *Eastb* —6D **14**
Quinnell Dri. *Hail* —5D **2**
Quintins, The. *Hail* —1E **5**
Quintin Way. *Hail* —4C **4**

Raglan Ct. *Pev* —6A **10**
Rainey Ct. *Eastb*
—4B **18** (1G **23**)
Raleigh Clo. *Eastb* —1E **19**
Ramsey Way. *Eastb* —6E **15**
Ranelagh Ct. *Eastb* —1E **19**
Rangemore Dri. *Eastb* —6F **13**
Ranworth Clo. *Eastb* —1B **14**
Rapson's Rd. *Eastb* —2B **12**
Rattle Rd. *Sto X & W'ham*
—6B **8**
Ratton Dri. *Eastb* —6D **12**
Ratton Gdns. *Eastb* —6D **12**
Ratton Rd. *Eastb* —3G **17**
Ravens Ct. *Eastb* —1H **21**
Ravens Cft. *Eastb* —1H **21**
Rectory Clo. *Eastb* —4F **17**
Redford Clo. *Eastb* —4E **15**
Redman King Ho. *Eastb*
—5H **17** (4C **22**)
Redoubt Rd. *Eastb* —3C **18**
Reedham Rd. *Eastb* —1B **14**
Regency Ct. *Eastb* —1H **21**
Regnum Clo. *Eastb* —1G **13**
Renfrew Ct. *Eastb* —1D **18**
(off Allfrey Rd.)
Residence, The. *Eastb* —1H **23**
Reynolds Rd. *Eastb* —4E **15**
Reynoldstown La. *Pol* —5B **6**
Richmond Pl. *Eastb*
—4H **17** (1C **22**)
Richmond Rd. *Pev B* —4B **10**
Ridgelands Clo. *Eastb* —4E **17**
Ridgeway, The. *Fris* —2A **20**
Ringmer Way. *Eastb* —1A **14**
Ringwood Clo. *Eastb* —2B **18**
Ringwood Ct. *Eastb* —2C **18**
Ringwood Rd. *Eastb* —2A **18**
Ripley Chase. *Eastb*
—4G **17** (1B **22**)
Ripsley Clo. *Eastb* —3E **15**
Rise Pk. Gdns. *Eastb* —3D **14**
Rising, The. *Eastb* —3D **14**
Riverbourne Ho. *Eastb*
—3B **18** (1H **23**)

Robert Ho. *Eastb* —3H **17**
(off Enys Rd.)
Robin Clo. *Eastb* —3C **14**
Robin Post La. *Pol* —1A **6**
Robinson Ct. *Eastb* —1C **18**
Roborough Clo. *Eastb* —3A **18**
Rochester Clo. *Eastb* —1E **21**
Rockall Dri. *Hail* —5C **2**
Rockhall Av. *Eastb* —5F **15**
Rockhurst Dri. *Eastb* —1D **16**
Rodmill Dri. *Eastb* —2F **17**
Rodmill Rd. *Eastb* —2F **17**
Rodmill Roundabout. *Eastb*
—1G **17**
Rodney Clo. *Eastb* —6E **15**
Roffrey Av. *Eastb* —4F **13**
Romans Way. *W'ham* —5E **9**
Romney Rd. *Pol* —5D **6**
Romney St. *Eastb* —2C **18**
Rookery, The. *Eastb* —1C **14**
Rope Wlk. *Eastb* —1D **4**
Rosebery Av. *Eastb* —4G **13**
Rosedale Pl. *Eastb* —2F **13**
(in two parts)
Roselands Av. *Eastb* —1C **18**
Roselands Clo. *Eastb* —2C **18**
Rosemullion. *Eastb* —6B **22**
Rosetti Rd. *Pev B* —5A **10**
Roseveare Rd. *Eastb* —1C **18**
Rother Av. *Sto X* —6H **7**
Rotherfield Av. *Eastb* —1A **14**
Rotunda Rd. *Eastb* —5D **14**
Rowan Av. *Eastb* —2F **13**
Rowsley Rd. *Eastb* —2F **21**
Roxburgh Ct. *Eastb* —2D **14**
Royal Pde. *Eastb*
—4C **18** (1H **23**)
Royal Sovereign Vw. *Eastb*
—1F **19**
Royal Sussex Cres. *Eastb*
—2D **16**
Royston Clo. *Fris* —2A **20**
Rush Ct. *Eastb*
—4B **18** (1G **23**)
Rushlake Cres. *Eastb* —1F **17**
Ruskin Rd. *Eastb* —4D **12**
Rusper Ho. *Eastb* —1B **22**
Rusper Rd. *Eastb* —1D **16**
Russet Clo. *Pol* —5E **7**
Rustington Ct. *Eastb*
—1H **21** (6D **22**)
Rutland Clo. *Eastb* —1F **17**
Rutland Ct. *Eastb* —4E **15**
Ruxley Ct. *Eastb* —3D **14**
Rydal Way. *Eastb* —1B **14**
Rye Clo. *Pol* —4E **7**
Ryefield Clo. *Eastb* —6E **13**
Rye St. *Eastb* —1D **18**
Rylstone Rd. *Eastb* —3C **18**

Sackville Rd. *Eastb* —3H **13**
Sackville Rd. *Hail* —3E **5**
Saffrons Ct. *Eastb*
—5G **17** (4B **22**)
Saffrons Ga. *Eastb*
—5H **17** (4C **22**)
Saffrons Mead. *Eastb*
—5H **17** (4C **22**)
Saffrons Pk. *Eastb*
—6G **17** (5B **22**)
Saffrons Rd. *Eastb*
—4G **17** (2B **22**)
St Andrews Clo. *Hail* —6C **2**
St Anne's Rd. *Eastb*
—3G **17** (1C **22**)
St Annes Rd. *Will* —2D **12**
St Anthony's Av. *Eastb* —5E **15**

St Aubyn's Rd. *Eastb*
—4B **18** (1H **23**)
St Boswells Clo. *Hail* —1C **4**
St Brelades. *Eastb* —4G **23**
St Clements Ct. *Eastb* —1F **17**
St Davids Clo. *Eastb* —1F **13**
St Denys. *Eastb* —3G **17**
St Georges. *Eastb* —3E **17**
St George's Rd. *Eastb*
—3B **18** (1H **23**)
St Gregory Clo. *Eastb*
—1G **21** (6A **22**)
St Helena Ct. *Eastb* —3G **17**
St James Rd. *Eastb* —3C **18**
St John's Dri. *W'ham* —5E **9**
St Johns Ho. *Eastb* —6C **22**
St John's Rd. *Eastb*
—1G **21** (6D **22**)
St John's Rd. *Pol* —5C **6**
St Kilda Mans. *Eastb* —1C **22**
St Leonard's Pl. *Eastb* —4E **17**
St Leonard's Rd. *Eastb*
—4H **17** (2D **22**)
St Leonards Ter. *Pol* —4B **6**
St Martins Rd. *Eastb* —2F **13**
St Mary's Av. *Hail* —2E **5**
St Mary's Clo. *Will* —3D **12**
St Marys Ct. *Eastb*
—4F **17** (1A **22**)
St Mary's Rd. *Eastb* —3F **17**
St Mellion Clo. *Hail* —1B **4**
St Michaels Clo. *Sto X* —5A **8**
St Nicholas Clo. *Pev* —5H **9**
St Paul's Clo. *Eastb* —2F **13**
St Philips Av. *Eastb* —2B **18**
St Ritas. *Eastb* —6F **17** (6A **22**)
St Vincents Pl. *Eastb*
—6G **17** (6A **22**)
St Wilfred's Grn. *Hail* —1E **5**
Salehurst Rd. *Eastb* —4E **17**
Salisbury Clo. *Eastb* —3E **13**
Salisbury Rd. *Eastb* —1E **21**
Salvador Clo. *Eastb* —6F **15**
Sancroft Rd. *Eastb* —4D **16**
Sanctuary, The. *Eastb* —3D **16**
Sandbanks Clo. *Hail* —4C **4**
Sandbanks Gdns. *Hail* —4D **4**
Sandbanks Gro. *Hail* —3D **4**
Sandbanks Rd. *Hail* —3C **4**
Sandbanks Way. *Hail* —3D **4**
Sandown Clo. *Eastb* —1A **14**
Sandpiper Wlk. *Eastb* —3C **14**
Sandwich St. *Eastb* —1C **18**
Sanshaw Ct. *Eastb*
—4G **17** (1A **22**)
Santa Cruz Dri. *Eastb* —6F **15**
Saxby Clo. *Eastb* —4E **15**
Saxon Pl. *Eastb* —1E **17**
Sayerland La. *Pol* —3C **6**
Sayerland Rd. *Pol* —4B **6**
Scanlon Clo. *Eastb* —2C **12**
Schofield Way. *Eastb* —6F **15**
School La. *Pol* —4C **6**
Seabeach La. *Eastb* —2C **18**
Seaford Rd. *Eastb* —2C **18**
Seaforth Ct. *Eastb* —4E **17**
Sea Rd. *Pev B* —4B **10**
Seaside. *Eastb* —4B **18** (1H **23**)
Seaside Rd. *Eastb*
—5B **18** (3G **23**)
Seaside Roundabout. *Eastb*
—6D **14**
Seaville Dri. *Eastb* —5D **14**
Seaville Dri. *Pev B* —4B **10**
Selby Rd. *Eastb* —2F **17**
Selmeston Ho. *Eastb* —3F **17**
Selmeston Rd. *Eastb* —6E **13**
Selsfield Clo. *Eastb* —1F **17**

Selwyn Dri. *Eastb* —3G **17**
Selwyn Ho. *Eastb* —3G **17**
Selwyn Pk. Ct. *Eastb* —3G **17**
Selwyn Rd. *Eastb*
—3G **17** (1B **22**)
Sevenoaks Rd. *Eastb* —3B **14**
Seven Sisters Rd. *Eastb*
—2D **12**
Shakespeare Wlk. *Eastb*
—3E **15**
Shalfleet Clo. *Eastb* —2B **14**
Shanklin Clo. *Eastb* —1B **14**
Shannon Way. *Eastb* —5F **15**
Sheen Rd. *Eastb*
—3B **18** (1H **23**)
Sheffield Pk. Way. *Eastb*
—1A **14**
Shelley Wlk. *Eastb* —3E **15**
Shepham La. *Pol* —4E **7**
Shepherds Clo. *Eastb* —2H **13**
Sheppey Wlk. *Hail* —4C **2**
Sheraton Clo. *Eastb*
—5H **17** (4D **22**)
Sherborne Ct. *Eastb* —3F **17**
(off Upperton Rd.)
Sherwood Ct. *Eastb* —3F **23**
Sherwood Grn. *Hail* —3D **4**
Shinewater Ct. *Eastb* —2B **14**
Shinewater La. *Eastb* —2B **14**
Shinewater Roundabout. *Eastb*
—4B **14**
Shipley Mill Clo. *Sto X* —6B **8**
Short Brow Clo. *Eastb* —2D **12**
Shortdean Pl. *Eastb* —3F **17**
Shortlands Clo. *Eastb* —4E **13**
Shropshire Ct. *Eastb* —6D **12**
Sidcup Clo. *Eastb* —3D **14**
Sidley Rd. *Eastb* —3C **18**
Silverdale Ct. *Eastb*
—6H **17** (6D **22**)
Silverdale Ct. *Hail* —1D **4**
Silverdale Rd. *Eastb*
—6G **17** (6B **22**)
Singleton Mill Rd. *Sto X* —6C **8**
Slindon Cres. *Eastb* —4E **15**
(in two parts)
Snowdon Clo. *Eastb* —2D **14**
Solly Ct. *Eastb* —1G **23**
Solway. *Hail* —5C **2**
Somerset Ct. *Eastb* —4E **15**
Somerville Clo. *Eastb* —6E **15**
Sorrel Clo. *Eastb* —2C **14**
Sorrel Dri. *Eastb* —1B **14**
Southampton Clo. *Eastb*
—5F **15**
South Av. *Eastb* —2D **16**
Southbourne Rd. *Eastb*
—1C **18**
South Cliff. *Eastb*
—1H **21** (6D **22**)
S. Cliff Av. *Eastb*
—6H **17** (6D **22**)
S. Cliff Tower. *Eastb* —1H **21**
South Clo. *Hail* —3D **4**
South Clo. *Pev B* —3D **10**
Southdown Av. *Eastb* —2C **12**
Southdown Cotts. *Eastb*
—2C **12**
Southdown Ho. *Eastb*
—6H **17** (6D **22**)
Southdown Rd. *Eastb* —6D **12**
South Elms *Eastb* —6B **22**
Southerden Clo. *Hail* —2E **5**
Southern Av. *Pol* —5D **6**
Southern Rd. *Eastb* —3H **13**
Southfield. *Pol* —6B **6**
Southfields Ct. *Eastb*
—4H **17** (2C **22**)

Southfields Rd. *Eastb*
—4G **17** (1B **22**)
S. Lynn Dri. *Eastb* —3H **17**
South Rd. *Hail* —3C **4**
South St. *Eastb* —3D **22**
(in two parts)
South Vw. *Eastb* —3G **17**
Sovereign Ct. *Eastb* —2C **18**
Sovereign Ho. *Eastb* —4G **23**
Spencer Ct. *Eastb* —4E **23**
Spencer Ho. *Eastb* —4E **23**
Spencer Rd. *Eastb*
—5A **18** (4E **23**)
Spring Clo. *Eastb* —4D **12**
Springfield Clo. *W'ham* —5F **9**
Springfield Rd. *Eastb* —3B **18**
Spring Lodge Clo. *Eastb*
—3E **15**
Spruce Clo. *Eastb* —3F **13**
Spur Rd. *Pol* —6D **6**
Spurway Pk. *Pol* —6D **6**
Squab La. *Hail* —2H **3**
Square, The. *Pev B* —3D **10**
Stables La. *Eastb*
—5A **18** (2E **23**)
Stafford Ct. *Eastb* —4E **15**
(off Etchingham Rd.)
Stafford Ho. *Eastb*
—4H **17** (2D **22**)
Stanhope Ct. *Eastb* —6C **22**
Stanley Rd. *Eastb* —3B **18**
Stanmer Dri. *Eastb* —4F **13**
Stanmer Ho. *Eastb*
—5H **17** (4D **22**)
Stansted Rd. *Eastb* —3A **18**
Stanton Prior. *Eastb* —1F **21**
Star Rd. *Eastb* —4G **17** (1A **22**)
Station App. *Eastb* —4H **13**
Station Pde. *Eastb* —2D **22**
Station Rd. *Hail* —2D **4**
Station Rd. *Hell* —2B **2**
Station Rd. *Pol* —4C **6**
Station Rd. Ind. Est. *Hail* —3E **5**
Station Roundabout. *Eastb*
—4H **17** (2D **22**)
Station St. *Eastb*
—4A **18** (2D **22**)
Staveley Rd. *Eastb* —1G **21**
Steeple Grange. *Eastb* —3G **17**
Stevenson Clo. *Eastb* —2E **15**
Stiles, The. *Hail* —2E **5**
Stirling Ct. *Eastb* —4E **15**
Stonegate Clo. *Eastb* —1A **14**
Stoney Down. Eastb —1G **21**
(off Milnthorpe Rd.)
Stoney La. *Hail* —2E **5**
Stringwalk, The. *Hail* —2E **5**
Stroma Clo. *Hail* —5B **2**
Stuart Av. *Eastb* —1E **17**
Sturdee Clo. *Eastb* —6F **15**
Sturton Pl. *Hail* —2D **4**
Suffolk Ct. *Eastb* —3C **18**
Sumach Clo. *Eastb* —3G **13**
Summer Ct. *Eastb* —2F **21**
Summer Ct. *Hail* —1D **4**
Summerdown Clo. *Eastb*
—4F **17**
Summerdown La. *E Dean*
—2C **20**
Summerdown Rd. *Eastb*
—4E **17**
Summerfields Av. *Hail* —1C **4**
Summerheath Rd. *Hail* —1D **4**
Summerlands Rd. *Eastb*
—3D **12**
Sunningdale Clo. *Hail* —6C **2**
Sun Patch. *Hail* —2E **5**
Sunset Clo. *Pev B* —3C **10**

Sunstar La. *Pol* —5A **6**
Susan's Rd. *Eastb*
—4A **18** (1F **23**)
Sussex Av. *Hail* —1D **4**
Sussex Clo. *Hail* —1D **4**
Sussex Ct. *Eastb* —2B **18**
Sussex Gdns. *E Dean* —2C **20**
Sussex Ho. *Eastb* —3F **23**
Sutton Ho. *Eastb* —6B **22**
Sutton Rd. *Eastb*
—4A **18** (2E **23**)
Swale Clo. *Pev* —6A **8**
Swallow Clo. *Eastb* —3B **14**
Swan Bus. Cen. *Hail* —3F **5**
Swanley Clo. *Eastb* —3D **14**
Swan Rd. *Hail* —3E **5**
Swinburne Av. *Eastb* —2D **12**
Sycamore Clo. *Eastb* —2F **13**
Sycamore Dri. *Hail* —3D **4**
Sycamores, The. *Eastb* —3H **17**
Sydney Rd. *Eastb*
—4B **18** (1G **23**)

Taddington Ho. *Eastb* —3C **18**
(off Taddington Rd.)
Taddington Rd. *Eastb* —3C **18**
Tamarack Clo. *Eastb* —3F **13**
Tamar Clo. *Pev* —6A **8**
Tanbridge Rd. *Eastb* —3F **15**
Tanneries, The. *Mag D* —3H **3**
Tas Combe Way. *Eastb* —3D **12**
Tavistock. *Eastb* —4F **23**
Tavistock. *Eastb*
—5A **18** (4F **23**)
(off Devonshire Pl.)
Telscombe Rd. *Eastb* —3F **15**
Tennis Clo. *Hail* —2D **4**
Tennyson Wlk. *Eastb* —2E **15**
Tenterden Clo. *Eastb* —3D **14**
Terminus Pl. Hail —2E **5**
(off Station Rd.)
Terminus Rd. *Eastb*
—4A **18** (2E **23**)
(in three parts)
Thackeray Clo. *Eastb* —2E **15**
Thatchings, The. *Pol* —6C **6**
Thorn Lodge. *Eastb* —4E **23**
Thornton Ct. *Eastb*
—4B **18** (1G **23**)
Thornwood. *Eastb*
—4H **17** (1D **22**)
Thornwood Clo. *Eastb* —3G **13**
Thorpe, The. *Eastb*
—6H **17** (6C **22**)
Thurrock Clo. *Eastb* —2C **12**
Tidebrook Gdns. *Eastb* —3F **15**
Tideswell Rd. *Eastb*
—4A **18** (2F **23**)
Tilehurst Dri. *Hail* —1C **4**
Tilgate Clo. *Eastb* —6F **13**
Tillingham Clo. *Sto X* —6A **8**
Tillingham Way. *Sto X* —6A **8**
Timberlaine Rd. *Pev B* —5A **10**
Timberley Rd. *Eastb* —4F **13**
Timbers Ct. *Hail* —2E **5**
Tintern Clo. *Eastb* —2G **13**
Tolkien Rd. *Eastb* —3F **15**
Tollgate Gdns. *Eastb* —6D **14**
Torfield Clo. *Eastb* —3G **17**
Torfield Rd. *Eastb* —3G **17**
Tott Yew Rd. *Eastb* —1C **12**
Tovey Clo. *Eastb* —1F **17**
Tower Clo. *Pev B* —2D **10**
Tower Mill Pl. *Pol* —6C **6**
Trafalgar M. *Eastb* —3C **18**
Treemaines Rd. *Eastb* —3F **15**
Triangle, The. *Eastb* —2C **12**

Trinity Pl.—Youl Grange

Trinity Pl. *Eastb*
—5A **18** (3F **23**)
Trinity Trees. *Eastb*
—5A **18** (3F **23**)
Troon Cotts. *Hail* —1B **4**
Trossachs Clo. *Eastb* —2D **14**
Tudor Ct. *Eastb*
—6H **17** (5D **22**)
Tugwell Rd. *Eastb* —3H **13**
Turnberry Dri. *Hail* —1C **4**
Turner Clo. *Eastb* —4D **14**
Tutts Barn Ct. *Eastb* —2H **17**
(off Tutts Barn La.)
Tutts Barn La. *Eastb* —2H **17**
Tweedsmuir Clo. *Eastb* —2C **14**
Twineham Rd. *Eastb* —6F **13**
Tyrone Ct. *Eastb* —4D **14**

Union Clo. *Hail* —4D **2**
Upland Rd. *Eastb* —5D **16**
Upper Av. *Eastb*
—3A **18** (1E **23**)
Upper Av. Roundabout. *Eastb*
—3A **18** (1E **23**)
Up. Carlisle Rd. *Eastb* —1E **21**
Up. Duke's Dri. *Eastb* —2E **21**
Up. Horsebridge Rd. *Hail*
—4A **2**
Up. King's Dri. *Eastb* —4D **12**
Up. Ratton Dri. *Eastb* —5D **12**
Upper St. *E Dean* —3B **20**
Upperton Gdns. *Eastb*
—4H **17** (1C **22**)
Upperton La. *Eastb*
—4H **17** (1C **22**)
Upperton Rd. *Eastb*
—3G **17** (1B **22**)
Up. Wish Hill. *Eastb* —5D **12**
Upwick Rd. *Eastb* —4E **17**
Upwyke Ho. *Eastb* —3E **17**

Valentine Ct. *Eastb* —3E **23**
Val Prinseps Rd. *Pev B* —5A **10**
Vega Clo. *Hail* —2F **5**
Veitch Ter. *Eastb* —2D **16**
Ventnor Clo. *Eastb* —1B **14**
Vernon Clo. *Eastb* —6E **15**
Vernon Lodge. *Eastb* —4E **23**
Vian Av. *Eastb* —6F **15**
Vicarage Dri. *Eastb* —4F **17**
Vicarage Field. *Hail* —1E **5**
Vicarage La. *Eastb* —4F **17**
Vicarage La. *Hail* —1E **5**
Vicarage La. *Hell* —1C **2**
Vicarage Rd. *Eastb*
—4F **17** (1A **22**)
Vicarage Rd. *Hail* —2E **5**
Victoria Clo. *Pol* —4B **6**

Victoria Ct. *Eastb*
—5A **18** (4F **23**)
Victoria Dri. *Eastb* —1E **17**
Victoria Gdns. *Eastb* —3D **16**
Victoria Mans. *Eastb* —3G **23**
Victoria Rd. *Eastb* —2D **16**
Victoria Rd. *Hail* —2E **5**
Victoria Rd. *Pol* —4B **6**
Viking Way. *Eastb* —5F **15**
Village, The. *Eastb* —1F **21**
Vincent Clo. *Eastb* —6F **15**
Vineries, The. *Eastb* —4D **14**
Vine Sq. *Eastb* —1D **18**
Vintry, The. *Eastb* —6E **13**

Wade Clo. *Eastb* —6F **15**
Wadey Pl. *Hail* —2F **5**
Wadhurst Clo. *Eastb* —3H **13**
Waldron Clo. *Eastb* —5F **13**
Walford Ho. *Eastb* —6C **22**
Walker Clo. *Eastb* —6F **15**
Waller Ct. *Pev* —3D **10**
Wallis Av. *Eastb* —5E **15**
Wallis Pl. *Eastb* —5E **15**
Wallsend Rd. *Pev B* —5H **9**
Walnut Tree Wlk. *Eastb* —5D **12**
Walnut Wlk. *Pol* —5C **6**
Walpole Wlk. *Eastb* —2E **15**
Walsingham Clo. *Eastb* —2F **13**
Walton Clo. *Eastb* —2E **15**
Wannock Av. *Eastb* —1B **12**
Wannock Dri. *Pol* —6B **6**
Wannock Gdns. *Pol* —2B **12**
Wannock La. *Eastb* —2B **12**
Wannock Rd. *Eastb* —2D **18**
Wannock Rd. *Pol* —1B **12**
Warburton Clo. *Eastb* —5E **13**
Warminster Rd. *Pev B* —4B **10**
Warren Clo. *Eastb* —1E **21**
Warren Clo. *E Dean* —2B **20**
Warren La. *Fris* —2B **20**
Warrior Ho. *Eastb* —1G **21**
Warrior Sq. *Eastb* —3C **18**
Wartling Rd. *Eastb* —1C **18**
Warwick Clo. *Amb* —4E **3**
Warwick Ct. *Eastb* —4E **15**
Watermill Clo. *Pol* —6C **6**
Waterworks Rd. *Eastb* —3A **18**
Watts La. *Eastb*
—3G **17** (1A **22**)
Waverley Gdns. *Pev B* —4B **10**
Wayford Clo. *Eastb* —3D **14**
Wayside. *E Dean* —3B **20**
Wealden Rd. *Eastb* —4E **13**
Weatherby Clo. *Eastb* —5E **13**
Wedderburn Rd. *Eastb* —4D **12**
Welbeck Clo. *Eastb* —2F **13**
(in two parts)
Wellcombe Cres. *Eastb* —2F **21**

Wellesley Rd. *Eastb*
—4A **18** (1F **23**)
Wellington Ct. *Eastb* —2C **18**
(off Roselands Av.)
Wellsbourne Rd. *Pev* —6A **8**
Wells Clo. *Eastb* —1E **21**
Wenthill Clo. *E Dean* —2B **20**
Went Hill Gdns. *Eastb* —2D **12**
Went Way. *E Dean* —3B **20**
Wentworth Clo. *Hail* —6C **2**
Wentworth Ct. *Eastb* —1E **19**
Westcliffe Ct. *Eastb* —6D **22**
Westcliff Mans. *Eastb* —6D **22**
West Clo. *Pol* —4D **6**
Westdown Rd. *Eastb* —3F **23**
Westerham Rd. *Eastb* —4D **14**
Western Av. *Pol* —5D **6**
Western Rd. *Eastb* —3B **18**
Western Rd. *Hail* —1C **4**
Western Rd. *Pev B* —5B **10**
Westfield Clo. *Pol* —4C **6**
Westfield Ct. *Pol* —5C **6**
Westfield Rd. *Eastb* —1F **17**
Westham Dri. *Pev B* —3D **10**
West Ho. *Eastb* —5A **18** (4E **23**)
Westminster Clo. *Eastb* —1F **13**
Westmorland Ct. *Eastb* —6D **12**
West St. *Eastb* —5H **17** (3D **22**)
West St. M. *Eastb* —3D **22**
West Ter. *Eastb*
—5H **17** (2D **22**)
Wexford Ct. *Eastb* —4D **14**
(off Biddenden Clo.)
Wharf Rd. *Eastb*
—4H **17** (2D **22**)
Wheelwright Clo. *Eastb* —1F **13**
Whiffens Clo. *Hail* —3C **4**
Whitbread Clo. *Eastb* —1B **14**
White Gables. *Eastb*
—6H **17** (5D **22**)
Whitley Rd. *Eastb* —3A **18**
Whittle Dri. *Eastb* —4A **14**
Wicklow Ct. *Eastb* —4D **14**
(off Biddenden Clo.)
Wildwood. *Eastb* —1C **14**
Willard Clo. *Eastb* —1A **18**
Williams Ct. *Eastb* —4E **15**
Willingdon Clo. *Eastb* —4D **12**
Willingdon Ct. *Eastb* —2C **12**
Willingdon Drove. *Eastb*
—4A **14**
Willingdon Pk. Dri. *Eastb*
—3E **13**
Willingdon Rd. *Eastb* —4E **13**
(in two parts)
Willingdon Roundabout. *Eastb*
—5E **13**
Willingdon Way. *Eastb* —3D **12**
Willoughby Cres. *Eastb* —1C **18**
Willow Av. *Hail* —6D **2**

Willow Down Clo. *Pol* —6C **6**
Willow Dri. *Pol* —6C **6**
Willowfield Rd. *Eastb*
—4B **18** (1H **23**)
Willowfield Sq. *Eastb*
—4B **18** (1H **23**)
Willow Wlk. *Eastb* —3F **13**
Wilmington Gdns. *Eastb*
—6A **18** (5E **23**)
Wilmington Sq. *Eastb*
—6A **18** (5E **23**)
Wilton Av. *Eastb* —2H **13**
Wiltshire Ct. *Eastb* —4E **15**
Winchcombe Rd. *Eastb*
—3A **18** (1F **23**)
Winchelsea Rd. *Eastb* —1D **18**
Winchester Ho. *Eastb* —2G **13**
Winchester Way. *Eastb* —3D **12**
Windermere Ct. *Eastb* —3F **23**
Windermere Cres. *Eastb*
—2C **18**
Windmill Clo. *Eastb* —1F **17**
Windmill Clo. *Pev* —6F **9**
Windmill Grn. *Sto X* —6C **8**
Windmill La. *Fris* —2A **20**
Windmill Pl. *Pol* —6B **6**
Windmill Rd. *Pol* —6C **6**
Windover Way. *Eastb* —2D **12**
Windsor Clo. *Eastb* —2C **14**
Windsor Ct. *Eastb*
—4B **18** (1H **23**)
Windsor Rd. *Hail* —3D **4**
Windsor Way. *Pol* —4C **6**
Winkney Rd. *Eastb* —2H **13**
Winston Cres. *Eastb* —6D **14**
Wish Hill. *Eastb* —4D **12**
Wish Rd. *Eastb* —5A **18** (3E **23**)
Withyham Clo. *Eastb* —4H **13**
Woburn Clo. *Hail* —6C **2**
Woburn Way. *Eastb* —2F **13**
Woodcroft Dri. *Eastb* —6E **13**
Woodgate Rd. *Eastb* —2B **18**
Woodland Av. *Eastb* —5E **13**
Woodlands Clo. *Hail* —5E **3**
Woodpecker Dri. *Hail* —1C **4**
Woodpecker Rd. *Eastb* —3B **14**
Woodside Way. *Hail* —5C **4**
Woodward Clo. *Eastb* —6E **15**
Wordsworth Dri. *Eastb* —3E **15**
Wren Pl. *Eastb* —1C **12**
Wrestwood Av. *Eastb* —4E **13**
Wrotham Clo. *Eastb* —4D **14**
Wroxham Rd. *Eastb* —1B **14**

Yieldings Clo. *Eastb* —2F **17**
York Rd. *Eastb*
—5H **17** (3D **22**)
Yorkshire Ct. *Eastb* —6D **12**
Youl Grange. *Eastb* —6F **17**